RHETORIC AND CRITICISM

Rhetoric and Criticism

MARIE HOCHMUTH NICHOLS

Louisiana State University Press

BATON ROUGE

PN
175
·N5

ISBN 0-8071-0122-2 (paper)
ISBN 0-8071-0630-5 (cloth)
Library of Congress Catalog Card Number 63-7958
Copyright © 1963 by Louisiana State University Press
Manufactured in the United States of America
1972 printing

Introduction

Professor Marie Hochmuth Nichols' lectures concern rhetoric, public address, and rhetorical criticism, or to put it another way—theory, practice, and judgment in speaking. In this context the word *rhetoric* may confuse and even disturb readers for whom its connotations are derogatory. As a symbol, this word carrying its "hodge-podge of conceptions," has often been misunderstood, misused, and even maligned. At the outset we should clearly understand how Professor Nichols uses the term. Of course she is not discussing the teaching of high school or college composition or the use of extravagant or bombastic language. Instead, she is thinking of rhetoric as a traditional concept, applying to the theory of speechmaking.

Some writers distinguish between the old rhetoric and the new rhetoric. For example, I. A. Richards in his *The Philosophy of Rhetoric* (1936) argues that "the old" started with Aristotle and ended with Richard Whately, who wrote *The Elements of Rhetoric* (1828). In this traditional sense, the term refers to the total art of public speaking and to its several aspects, viz., invention, arrangement, style, memory, and delivery. Limiting the field considerably, Richards believes that the new rhetoric "should be a study of misunderstanding and its remedies" or a study of "how words work in discourse." Other recent writers have different views of how to rescue the subject from its past.

How does Professor Nichols define rhetoric? She describes it as "the theory and the practice of the verbal mode of presenting judgment and choice, knowledge and feeling." She synthesizes the new and the old, recognizing what is valuable in older treatments, yet seeing also what is challenging and promising in the newer approaches.

What is Professor Nichols' scheme or plan of development? She sees her subject as a kaleidoscopic one, best viewed from different positions and in different lights. In the opening lecture she identifies "the study and the practice of oral discourse" as "a humane study," involving "the formation of judgment and choices." Here she sets forth a standard by which to measure speeches and speakers and by which to establish pedagogical goals and methods.

In the next four lectures, she explores the nature, methods, and limitations of rhetorical criticism. For example, in her second lecture she discusses "the alliance of history, rhetoric, and public address." Keenly aware of the objections which historians have leveled at rhetoricians, she reviews carefully and objectively those that are pertinent to recent rhetorical scholarship. Her observations and counsel in this area are made the more valuable because of her recent experience as the editor of the third volume of *The History and Criticism of American Public Address*.

In the third lecture, she analyzes "the grave implications of ghost writing," pointing out how the practice makes judgments difficult and tentative. The employment of a ghost writer disturbs the intimate relationship between thought and language and makes it difficult to assess the intellectual qualities, moral standards, and, of course, the style of the speaker.

After reviewing in the fourth lecture the approaches which anthologists and others have used in collecting and evaluating speeches, she moves in the fifth lecture toward answering the central question: "What is our nature as critics of speeches?" In her opinion "much of our difficulty comes . . . from failing to reconcile two fundamentally different traditional concepts of rhetoric, the Ciceronian tradition and the Renaissance tradition," or a rhetoric based upon the five canons and the Ramistic system which limited the subject to style and delivery. She is particularly concerned with the failure of modern rhetorical critics to take the responsibility for the assessment of the truth and relevance of statements and to give adequate attention to "word construction and images." She feels that they have been guilty of substituting "analytic jargon for analysis." It is in this discussion that Professor Nichols most forcefully brings to bear her knowledge and insight, not only on the recent and the traditional, but also on the superficial and the sound.

These first five lectures present a clear view of the emerging concepts of rhetorical criticism as a separate discipline. They put into perspective the forty-year struggle of rhetorical criticism to divorce itself from literary criticism, to determine its relationship to historiography, and to win a place in contemporary education as a humane study. At the same time they expose foibles and nearsightedness, thereby pointing the way to more mature methods and sharper judgments.

Moving to a new position in the sixth lecture, Professor Nichols engages in what she refers to as "Alpine climbing," a consideration of what Burke and Richards may contribute to rhetoric and criticism. Because she believes that present-day critics have been inept and fumbling in their attempts to describe and evaluate language and style, it is evident that she looks with favor upon Burke and Richards, "who," she says, "provide a stimulus and who may give promise of providing rhetoricians with a theory which is better adapted to learning and thought of modern times than any conception arrived at two thousand years ago for a culture quite different from our own." In the dual role of interpreter and critic, she perceptively finds her way through the new rhetorics, which some persons find abstruse and obscure, and presents what seems to be provocative and stimulating in numerous writings of these two scholars.

In the eighth and concluding lecture, Professor Nichols, taking some of her own medicine, turns critic and presents a study of the speaking of George Bernard Shaw. Her approach is mainly traditional although balanced with the modern influence. In any event, the sparkling analysis provides an example of what she believes should constitute rhetorical criticism.

Marie Hochmuth Nichols, Professor of Speech of the University of Illinois, delivered the present group of eight lectures at the Annual Conference on Speech Education at Louisiana State University in June, 1959. Subsequently the lectures were carefully revised and polished for publication. Fortunately in the process of reworking, Professor Nichols has retained throughout the spirit of her oral presentation.

Inaugurated in 1935, this conference lectureship has through the years brought to the Louisiana campus twenty-eight of the foremost speech educators. They have come from twenty-one different institutions; sixteen have been presidents of the Speech Association of America. The twenty-eight have represented varied areas of interest: ten coming from public address, five from speech education, three from interpretation, three from theater, three from speech correction, and one each from speech psychology, speech science, general semantics, and radio-television. Almost all have written significant monographs and distinguished books.

Beyond telling them to expect audiences composed of students, undergraduate and graduate, and faculty members with widely diverse interests, we have made little attempt to influence our lecturers' choice of subjects or sequence of presentation. We have simply invited to follow their interests and to share with us their latest observations, research, methods, philosophies, and experiences. The resultant variety has been stimulating and delightful.

We are much in the debt of all these persons who have given liberally of their time and insight and who have contributed to our enlightenment and inspiration. We regret that we have not made all of the contributions available to a wider audience through publication and present Professor Nichols' lectures as representative of the series.

WALDO W. BRADEN
Chairman, Department of Speech

Contents

RHETORIC AND CRITICISM

Chapter 1

Rhetoric
and Public Address
as Humane Study

I have been dubious about the subject of "Rhetoric and Public Address as Humane Study." It seems almost impossible these days to talk about humane study, or the humanities, without going into a deep Puritan gloom. How much of the gloom is real and how much of it is words without heart and will is difficult to determine. There are times when one seems to find a bit of snob-appeal in the matter of being gloomy about the plight of the humanities. You know how that runs: "I am gloomier than you are about the plight of the humanities"; or, "When you are as gloomy as I am, we will be able to talk seriously about the plight of the humanities."

Although the gloom deepened about the time Sputnik was launched, it did not, of course, begin then. It had been gathering for a very long time, easily since the beginning of the decline of classical studies in the nineteenth century. But that it is very deep now, can scarcely be gainsaid. In truth, it appears that even the staunchest allies of humane studies have been caught up in it. In a recent issue of *The Quarterly Journal of Speech*, a well-known friend of humane studies asked: "Should the student who is to be well educated in this time of appalling need for scientists be allowed to spend his time in debating about education?"[1] I do not know what you think of a question like this but I do not find in it an omen of good. When thoughtful activity is to be circumscribed by the need for scientists, I would suspect that we may no longer be thinking of the fully developed individual.

I do not believe gloom will alter the situation. Nor do I think that an assault on the growth of the sciences will alter it. If, upon examination, the humanities reveal unique values, there will be those who cultivate them, exhibit their values in their own lives, and assert their values abroad, hoping that by contagion, at least, they may serve others.

What one means by humane study is not always clear. Some of the same confusion seems to surround the word *humane* as surrounded the notion of Einstein's theory of relativity. Perhaps you are familiar with the charming story of Einstein's valiant attempt to make himself clear on his subject. While attending a party, the professor once was asked to describe his theory of relativity. "The best way I can do that," replied Einstein, "is to tell you of the time I asked a blind friend to have a drink of milk." "I know what a drink is," said the friend, "but what is milk?" "Milk is a white liquid," responded Einstein. "Liquid, I know," said his blind friend, "but what is white?" "The color of a swan's feathers," said Einstein. "I know what feathers are, but what is a swan?" "A swan," said Einstein, "is a bird with a crooked neck." "A neck, I know," said his blind friend, "but what is crooked?" Einstein took his friend's arm, so the story goes, and held it out. "That is straight," he said. Then he bent it and said, "That is crooked." "Ah!" exclaimed the blind man, "Now I know what milk is." "And that in a nutshell," Einstein told the party, "is my theory of relativity."

Definitions of the humanities have not always been any more enlightening, but I am sure most of them have not been quite so witty. If one turns to *Webster's New International Dictionary*, he finds that humanity 3b "Usually in *pl.* with *the*" means "the branches of polite learning regarded as primarily conducive to culture; esp., the ancient classics and belles-lettres; sometimes, secular, as distinguished from theological, learning." If one turns to the three page effort of the *New English Dictionary* to make *humane* and related words clear, he finds Humanity 4 to mean:

"learning or literature concerned with human culture: a term including the various branches of polite scholarship, as grammar, rhetoric, poetry, and esp. the study of the ancient Latin and Greek classics." If one seeks a world outlook and turns to the *New World Dictionary,* he finds under "the humanities": "1. language and literature, especially the classical Greek and Latin. 2. the branches of learning concerned with human thought and relations, as distinguished from the sciences; especially literature and philosophy, and, often, the fine arts, history, etc." Presumably one has the choice of separating himself, on the one hand, from God, and, on the other, from science, but what lies between is not entirely clear.

Where so much elusiveness abounds, one is not likely to feel himself much more enlightened than was Einstein's blind friend. Personally, I like the conception of the humanities presented by the distinguished American philosopher, Ralph Barton Perry. "I define 'the humanities,'" he says, "to embrace whatever influences conduce to freedom. 'The humanities,' is not to be employed as a mere class name for certain divisions of knowledge or parts of a scholastic curriculum, or for certain human institutions, activities and relationships, but to signify a certain condition of freedom which these may serve to create." And by "freedom," says Perry, ". . . I mean enlightened choice. I mean the action in which habit, reflex or suggestion are superseded by an individual's fundamental judgments of good and evil; the action whose premises are explicit; the action which proceeds from personal reflection and integration."[2] The definition, says Perry, is not unlike Montaigne's, contained in his essay "Of the Education of Children," where Montaigne explains a proper liberal education and suggests that the tutor make the pupil examine and thoroughly "sift everything" he reads, "and lodge nothing in his head upon a simple authority and trust. . . . Let not the principles of Aristotle," says Montaigne, "be principles to him, anymore than those of the Stoics and the Epicureans. Let this diversity of opinions be laid before him; he will choose, if he be able; if not, he will remain in doubt.[3] . . . We are not subjects of a king: let each one claim his own freedom."[4] Quoting Seneca, Montaigne goes on to observe, *"Who follows another, follows nothing. He finds nothing, nay, he seeks nothing."*[5] The pupil's "education, his labour and study, tend to nothing else but to form . . . [his judgment]."[6]

The story is told of Immanuel Kant that nine days before his death he was visited by his physician. Old, ill and nearly blind, he rose from his chair and stood trembling with weakness and muttering unintelligible words. Finally his faithful companion realized that he would not sit down again until the visitor had taken a seat. This he did, and Kant then permitted himself to be helped to his chair. After having regained some of his strength, he said, "Das Gefühl für Humanität hat mich noch nicht verlassen"—"The sense of humanity has not yet left me." The two men were moved almost to tears. Although the word *Humanität* had come, in the eighteenth century, to mean little more than politeness or civility, it had for Kant a much deeper significance, which the circumstances of the moment served to emphasize: "man's proud and tragic consciousness of self-approved and self-imposed principles, contrasting with his utter subjection to illness, decay and all that is implied in the word 'mortality.' "[7]

Everett Lee Hunt, Dean emeritus at Swarthmore College in Pennsylvania, has summed up the matter very well in characterizing the humanities. Like Perry, he sees humanistic study having as its concern judgment and enlightened choice. And an "enlightened choice" is for him "a choice based upon a wide knowledge of all the alternatives. . . ." But "knowledge about the alternatives is not enough. There must be imagination to envisage all the possibilities, and sympathy to make some of the options appeal to the emotions and powers of the will. Such dignity as man may have is achieved by the exercise of free choice through the qualities of learning, imagination, and sympathy; and we should add to these qualities as a fitting accompaniment, what may be called civility."[8]

Pico, the Italian humanist of the fifteenth century, said in his speech "On the Dignity of Man" that God placed man in the center of the universe so that he might be conscious of where he stands, and therefore free to decide "where to turn." Pico does not say that man *is* the center of the universe, not even in the sense of the classical phrase, "man the measure of all things."[9] Although the first choice that man made may have condemned all of us to bad choices the rest of our lives, nevertheless, we may be obligated to do the best we can under the circumstances. The speech of the serpent in the Garden of Eden may have in it a real lesson on the virtues of restraint and the importance of imagination in envisaging consequences.

I take humane studies, then, to be concerned with the formation of judgment and choice. When the Bell Telephone Company took a group of its employees to the University of Pennsylvania campus to study history, philosophy, logic, language, ethics, and literature, I believe it was saying that technical efficiency is not enough, that somewhere beyond that lies an area in which answers are not formulary and methods not routine. I believe it was saying that beyond the area of the formula lies an area where understanding, imagination, knowledge of alternatives, and a sense of purpose operate. That these studies made a difference may be found in the fact that after a year the lives of the individuals were so altered that they could no longer get along with their own families who performed on a different level; hence, thereafter, the families were also given the benefit of the opportunity for learning. I cannot believe that the service organization would continue the practice unless in the operations of the organization, decision-making manifested a different quality of judgment than it had previously. As one of the beneficiaries of the study testified, "This may not teach us to make decisions faster— or even as quickly—but they will be better decisions."[10]

If the idea of *humane study* is difficult to approach, I am not sure that making clear what *rhetoric* means is any easier. The hodge-podge of conceptions is all too well known. One may narrow the field by ruling out such a conception as that which makes rhetoric the mere blandishments of a prose piece, or excessive aesthetics. We may rule out, too, such modern notions as those which stretch the conception of rhetoric to mean such things as the power of the sun to invite one outdoors. Most people may be willing to place rhetoric with those arts which are concerned with words in some way or another. I take rhetoric to mean the theory and the practice of the verbal mode of presenting judgment and choice, knowledge and feeling. As persuasion, it works in the area of the contingent, where alternatives are possible. In poetic, it is the art of imaginative appeal; in scientific discourse, it is the means of so presenting truth as to

fix it clearly in the mind of the listener or reader. After years of
reiteration of the narrow Aristotelian definition that rhetoric is
the "faculty of observing in any given case the available means
of persuasion,"[11] I find the conception of the literary critic, Allen
Tate, refreshing. "By rhetoric I mean," says Tate, "the study and
the use of the figurative language of experience as the discipline
by means of which men govern their relations with one another
in the light of truth."[12] Grounded on the disciplines of grammar
and logic, it is to Tate the "study of the full language of experience, not the specialized languages of method."[13] In other words,
rhetoric is a process of so embodying truth as to govern relationships between men. It is a means of so ordering discourse as
to produce an effect on the listener or reader. Such ordering requires exactness, compelling vitality, and what Tate has called
"historical imagination."[14]

It is commonly agreed that all men learn something from the
experience of other men, however little it may be. Let me turn
to some examples of the application of rhetorical principles to
illustrate in a particular way the embodiment of humane values,
examples of judgments that are rational, sensitive, imaginative,
and compelling.

Picture with me for a moment three scenes, all of which the
rhetorician may turn to with profit in his concern with the matter
of choice and judgment. The first is in Philadelphia on September
17, 1787. For four months a convention has been meeting to decide, or try to decide, under what rule the country might place
itself. There was bitterness and contention, indifference, and
indecision, fatigue and obstreperousness, and no one was really
satisfied with the results of the deliberations. People were
anxious to go home. Benjamin Franklin, among the oldest of
the group—tired too—gave men a chance to ennoble themselves,
as he ennobled himself, when he made the moral choice to place
again his great prestige at the service of his country and induce
the men who were there to place their signatures of approval,
however reluctantly, on the constitution that had been drafted.
Notice the temper of the man who speaks, his awareness of alternatives, his standing with his fellowmen, and let us ask how
this judgment developed. "Mr. President," said Franklin:

I confess that there are several parts of this constitution which I do not at present approve, but I am not sure I shall never approve them: For having lived long, I have experienced many instances of being obliged by better information or fuller consideration, to change opinions even on important subjects, which I once thought right, but found to be otherwise. It is therefore that the older I grow, the more apt I am to doubt my own judgment, and to pay more respect to the judgment of others. . . .

Thus, I consent, Sir, to this Constitution because I expect no better, and because I am not sure, that it is not the best. The opinions I have had of its errors, I sacrifice to the public good. I have never whispered a syllable of them abroad. Within these walls they were born, and here they shall die. . . .

On the whole, Sir, I cannot help expressing a wish that every member of the Convention who may still have objections to it, would with me, on this occasion doubt a little of his own infallibility, and to make manifest our unanimity, put his name to this instrument.[15]

The second scene is one in the United States Senate on July 22, 1850, when Henry Clay attempted to adjust the differences between the North and the South at a time when the nation was to be torn apart. Ill, he came out of retirement to add his prestige and his wisdom to a cause more important than himself—and in minimizing man, he elevated him. "Mr. President," he said:

. . . what is an individual man? An atom, almost invisible without a magnifying glass—a mere speck upon the surface of the immense universe—not a second in time, compared to immeasurable, never-beginning, and never-ending eternity; a drop of water in the great deep, which evaporates and is borne off by the winds; a grain of sand, which is soon gathered to the dust from which it sprung. Shall a being so small, so petty, so fleeting, so evanescent, oppose itself to the onward march of a great nation, to subsist for ages and ages to come—oppose itself to that long line of posterity which, issuing from our loins, will endure during the existence of the world? Forbid it God! Let us look to our country and our cause, elevate ourselves to the dignity of pure and disinterested patriots, wise and enlightened statesmen, and save our country from all impending dangers. What if, in the march of this nation to greatness and power, we should be buried beneath the wheels that propel it onward. What are we—what is any man worth who is not ready and willing to sacrifice himself for the benefit of his country when it is necessary.[16]

The third scene is in New York at the meeting of the New England Society on December 21, 1886. There, the beloved Henry Grady of Atlanta called upon New England to make a decision, having already made one for himself, as symbol of the South: "Now," said Grady:

> . . . what answer has New England to this message? Will she permit the prejudices of war to remain in the hearts of the conquerors, when it has died in the hearts of the conquered? Will she transmit this prejudice to the next generation, that in their hearts which never felt the generous ardor of conflict it may perpetuate itself? Will she withhold, save in strained courtesy, the hand which straight from his soldier's heart Grant offered to Lee at Appomattox? Will she make the vision of a restored and happy people, which gathered above the couch of your dying captain, filling his heart with grace; touching his lips with praise, and glorifying his path to the grave— will she make this vision on which the last sign of his expiring soul breathed a benediction, a cheat and delusion? If she does, the South, never abject in asking for comradeship, must accept with dignity its refusal. . . . [17]

I find considerable humanizing value in the examples of men in their moments of decision, exercising a judgment, moral, rational, imaginative, and in the finest tradition of the human spirit. The examples I have cited all seem to me to reflect the kind of freedom and enlightened choice that Ralph Barton Perry was talking about, that "action in which habit, reflex or suggestion are superseded by an individual's fundamental judgments of good and evil; the action whose premises are explicit; the action which proceeds from personal reflection and integration." I have remembered for many years a remark made by Professor Herbert Wichelns of Cornell University. "Considerable light," he said, "goes up on human nature when you contemplate it in its moments of decision." The study of rhetorical discourse yields scores of examples of men in their most manly occupation, that of making decisions which ennoble them, and, in general, give insight into our own lives. There is the verbal portrait of Socrates discoursing on immortality while the jailer prepared the hemlock;

the image of Christ saying, "Father forgive them, for they know not what they do"; Lincoln in 1861 giving a nation the choice of ennobling itself. All these are part of the tradition and give direction to lives that are exposed to them. I like the statement of the poet Hesiod as Aristotle quotes him:

> Far best is he who knows all things himself;
> Good, he that hearkens when men counsel right;
> But he who neither knows, nor lays to heart
> Another's wisdom, is a useless wight.[18]

What is the relationship of the study and the practice of oral discourse to the humanities? I find a large part of the substance of the humanities in the examples that are provided of men in their best moments as men. It has been well said that "the speech as a form gives us a microcosm of humanity, a man in high thought and feeling, in a worthy cause, seeking, by his word-artistry, to make his audience know and care."[19] One may agree with Richard Murphy's lament: "In the best of the past speeches we have these experiences preserved as illuminations of man's experience, and of the best in human nature. It is a pity not to draw freely upon this heritage."[20]

What better way of observing the manliness of high character and wisdom than observing the judgment of a Churchill, articulated in his speeches in the darkest hours of the war—a total man in the context of events. What better way of getting insight into character than pondering an Adlai Stevenson articulating his feelings in a moment of defeat in the 1952 presidential election. What better way of understanding the fight against evil than reading the speeches of George Bernard Shaw, exercising the judgment of a free man, dedicated to the uplift of the country of his adoption, using words that stung the English conscience, or using humor to arouse collective attack on slums, filth, and low wages.

But one may say: How is one to be humanely educated through pondering the shoddiness of tyrants, or ne'er-do-wells, ill-prepared political incompetents and charlatans, merely talking at the drop of a hat? Well, they too are free men—and we need to learn what not to do and say as well as what to do and say. The choice is ours as free men. Nor must we expect excellence only in speeches, when it does not dominate in any other walk of life. Poets, painters, essayists do not create masterpieces only; politicians are not all statesmen; lawyers are not all Clarence Darrows or Learned Hands. Greece did not consist merely of Pericles, nor Rome of Cicero, nor the eighteenth century of Chathams and Burkes, any more than our time is made up only of the wisdom of the Nehrus, Churchills, and Stevensons.

How unfortunate for our schools to substitute the art of conducting a telephone conversation for a study of Edmund Burke on "Conciliation with America," or Daniel Webster's great debate with Hayne, or Woodrow Wilson's "Fourteen Points."

On the side of a bank in Athens, with cypress almost covering the entrance, there is a stone cavern, a forbidding looking cavern. One can stand on top of the Acropolis and spot the iron bars at the entrance, with the Pnyx nearby, where held sway the eloquence of Athens. Socrates was supposed to have been imprisoned in the cavern for misleading the young men of Athens. Two thousand years later visitors to Athens hunt out the spot, with the help of a little old lady who can call out "Socrates," even though she knows not a word of English. Visitors in our own country hunt out Gettysburg and Springfield to ponder and recall the discourse and the example of a man who knew and cared, just as visitors hunt out the memorials and recall the words of men who cared in Athens, in Rome, in the Place de la Concorde, or beside the Thames. What better way of liberating the human spirit than by recalling examples of liberated men to study the thoughts and feelings which guided them?

All of us, I think, are aware that the theoretical study of rhetoric was from the beginning the support and foundation of Greek learning. Included in the trivium and quadrivium, its function was to develop that most distinguishing of human features, rationality. The recent statement of Bess Sondel of the University of Chicago in her book, *The Humanity of Words,* is well taken: "We are born into an environment of words just as surely as we are born into an environment of weather." Sondel continues, "The environment of words determines, from our earliest sentient moments, the nature of the environment of ideas and ideals in which we shall live. Through words, our ideas and our ideals become crystallized—almost solidified. They endure as 'culture' and as 'principles'. . . ."[21] Within the liberal arts college today, one finds considerable neglect of the theoretical study of words. It is because of this negligence that one can sympathize with the valiant attempt of Allen Tate to restore that theoretical study. "The natural sciences," he says, "have a highpowered rationale of their daily conquests of nature. The social sciences have a slippery analogical metaphor to sustain their self-confidence. The humanities modestly offer the vision of the historical lump. This lump is tossed at the student mind, which is conceived as the miraculous combination of the *tabula rasa* and innate powers of understanding. In short, the humanities have no rationale. . . . [Thus] our modest capacity for true understanding is frustrated. For the true rationale of humanistic study is now what it has always been, even though now it is not only in decay, but dead. I allude to the arts of rhetoric."[22]

I assume that the theory of rhetoric has something to do with the logical, emotional, and ethical dimensions of language, and that close examination and study of these dimensions would be eminently rewarding in the understanding of human nature. The great student of French literature, Gilbert Chinard, has remarked: ". . . the study of style, enables one to gain an insight into the mind of another human being, much more accurately than graphology would reveal the character of a man."[23] If the testimony of the centuries to the importance of style as an index of the human spirit needs support, we could find it in an unsuspected source—from one of the great atomic scientists of the twentieth century. As J. Robert Oppenheimer has said:

> The problem of doing justice to the implicit, the imponderable and the unknown is, of course, not unique to politics. It is always with us in science, it is with us in the most trivial of personal affairs, and it is one of the great problems of writing and of all forms of art. The means by which it is solved is sometimes called style. It is style which complements affirmation with limitation and with humility; it is style which makes it possible to act effectively, but not absolutely; it is style which, in the domain of foreign policy, enables us to find a harmony between the pursuit of ends essential to us, and the regard for views, the sensibilities, the aspirations of those to

whom the problem may appear in another light; it is above all
style through which power defers to reason.[24]

Thus, in its simplest manifestation, style is a mode of ingratiation;[25] in its most complex aspect it is the "ultimate morality of
mind."[26] It is an index of a preference for good work. It is a
means by which we govern our relations with other men. It is,
as has been said by the great French naturalist, Buffon, ". . . the
man himself."[27]

If style is the man himself, then a close scrutiny of the details
of style should tell us what manner of man is doing the speaking,
or the writing, and in what relationship he conceives himself to
be with his audience. If it is style which complements affirma-
tion with limitations and with humility; if it is style which makes
it possible to act effectively, but not absolutely; if it is style which
in the domain of foreign policy enables us to find a harmony between the pursuit of ends essential to us and the regard for the
views, the sensibilities, the aspirations of those to whom the
problem appears in another light; if it is style through which
power defers to reason—then, to look to style for the manifestations of healthy states and unhealthy states, for understanding
and misunderstanding, must become an imperative for anyone
concerned with the implications of his art.[28]

I was sitting in my office one night when a former student
pounded at the door and asked to come in. He was quiet and
pale and clutched in his hand two sheets of paper, neatly typed—
a letter to the press. That morning he had encountered in the
press the report of an Illinois legislator who was opposing the
idea of removing the death penalty for murder for a trial period
of six years, and the legislator had argued that such a scheme
would be a "terrible blow" to law enforcement. Then, the legislator had asked the house: "Are we getting chicken—are we going
religious?" The student, white with indignation, turned to me
and said: "Are we to identify being 'religious' with 'going
chicken?' That's what the words say, don't they?" I was glad
that student had not merely skimmed the words in the speech
but had paused to see what they said, glad he had not raised the
question whether humor was effective, but raised the question
whether this was a logic and a prose befitting legislative halls.

I believe that student is a better young man for having made a theoretical study of rhetoric; I believe he has learned to understand that a close study of language yields information both about the mind of the user and the mind of the receiver and about the relationship in which they stand to each other. As Donald Bryant of the State University of Iowa has remarked: "The frauds we suffer under from the huckster and shyster, from the religious and political medicine men, and from the well-meaning social (and even educational) incompetents, derive much of their strength from the merely *superficial* familiarity of our educated citizens with the live use of language, for good and for ill, over the years and the centuries."[29] A distinguished American critic has recently gone so far as to locate most of his fears for the future of the United States in the disappearance of a fundamental resonance from the language of official pronouncement. "Certainly a nation so lacking in resonance that it can accept federal prose as a language capable of legislating human destinies," he argues, "is a nation part way to the door of darkness. Does any man seriously believe he can hope to discover who we are by reading the day's prose from Washington?"[30] We have all gone through a period in which *inebriate, communist, subversive, security risk, homosexual,* and *incompetent* meant *undesirable,* and therefore all meant approximately the same thing. We have, on my own campus, gone through a period in which support for the fluoridation of water meant sanction of the use of poison, and poison was synonymous with Communism; therefore, fluoridation was the work of Communists.

Theoretical study of rhetoric, close attention to the maneuvers of language are, in a sense, real safeguards of freedom, for who can be free to form judgments rationally, as a man, if he is unaware of the abuses to which language so readily lends itself?

There is a tendency among us, I believe, to think that now that the scientists have come to study language, the humane scholars may leave. This is obviously an egregious error. I respect scientific attitudes and methods, including the most rigidly controlled laboratory experiment that one may conduct in the field of rhetoric. I want to know every kind of fact I can obtain by any kind of method that will yield facts. But one cannot live

by facts alone, staples that they are. The rhetorician is in effect,
or ought to be, a critic of society. To be a social critic one needs
a set of values pertaining to the ends of society, the causes one
may ethically advance. Emerson demonstrated this in his judgment of Disraeli:

> Disraeli, the chiffonier, wastes all his talent on the House of Com-
> mons, for the want of character. He makes a smart cutting speech,
> really introduces new and important distinctions. . . . But he makes
> at last no impression, because the hearer asks, Who are you? What
> is dear to you? What do you stand for? And the speech and the
> speaker are silent, and silence is confession. A man who has been
> a man has foreground and background. His speech, be it never so
> good, is subordinate and the least part of him, and as this man has
> no planet under him, but only his shoes, the hearer infers that the
> ground of the present argument may be no wider.[31]

This kind of judgment grows out of concern for human *purpose*
and *end,* and scientists in the field of rhetoric cannot determine
these purposes and ends. Let freedom from ignorance make our
judgments better; let awareness of consequences be our guide.
Yet, in the last analysis, what our direction is to be must be determined by something other than science. What ideals we shall
strive for and try to implement are not scientific matters. As
Einstein once remarked: "Perfection of means and confusion of
aims seem . . . to characterize our age."[32]

I have just been reading a series of conclusions with reference
to what communication experimentation has established. I am
told that the organization of speeches is unimportant provided
tractable audiences are explicitly motivated and, in persuasive
messages, the strongest arguments are presented first. I am told
that emotional appeals should be avoided if the audience will
subsequently be exposed to counterpropaganda. I am told that
humor does not increase the effectiveness of a serious speech.
And I am told that a person's speech improvement is generally
more dependent upon the amount and kind of training in delivery
he receives and how many opportunities he had for public speaking than upon any other factors.[33]

In the last act of *Antony and Cleopatra,* Cleopatra is told that
only in dreams could there be such a perfect person as Antony.
She turns to her informer and says, "You lie."[34] Now, I do not

recommend turning to our rhetorical scientist and saying, "You lie," for I am sure that his facts are better than my guesses, and I am deeply grateful for them. I do not think it is "smart to be ignorant." But still there is the previous question for a free man. Now that I have the facts, what do I do with them? Should I seek out tractable audiences and exercise my penchant for disorder and disarray? Should I avoid emotional appeals if the audience to which I talk will subsequently be exposed to counter-propaganda? Should I eliminate humor in the speech which is intended to be serious? Should I rehearse pear-shaped vowels and never mind whether I have anything of any worth to say? Perhaps I could take this course and be rewarded by applause, attain my so-called ends, and be effective, that is, if I were not a person who believes that society can become better than it is.

If scientific study of language reveals that appeal to a low motive is more effective than to a high, we still should say with James A. Winans, "Appeal to the best sentiments in your hearers."[35] And we should have some notion of what is high and low. There is a higher principle of rhetoric than technical effectiveness. Milton, Carlyle, Emerson, and scores of others have practiced it. The late John Livingston Lowes said of the King James Version of the Bible: "Its phraseology has become part and parcel of our common tongue—bone of its bone and flesh of its flesh. Its rhythms and cadences, its turns of speech, its familiar imagery, its very words, are woven into the texture of our literature, prose and poetry alike. . . . The English of the Bible . . . is characterized not merely by a homely vigour and pithiness of phrase, but also by a singular nobility of diction and by a rhythmic quality which is, I think, unrivalled in its beauty."[36] The revisers of the King James Version were advised to make it "more readable for the American public of today,"[37] and undoubtedly a readability formula could be applied with some success, but who would argue that some nobility has not gone out of the prose of the Bible?

Of course, it is not merely a matter of how certain practices will affect society. We are all affected by the devices we may choose to practice. What happens to a respect for good work if one regularly presents his remarks in disarray and disorder? What happens to one's steady growth as a human being if he

attends more to the manner of remarks than to the matter? Will
society be better as a result of the empty effectiveness of individuals who compose it?

Science can be expected to continue to turn up facts, and
everyone should welcome the freedom from ignorance. But as our
scientists turn up these facts, there will be increasing demand for
the wise use of them, and this wise use will result from reason, imagination, good will, which, I believe, derive in part at least from a
humane approach to our subject. The humanities without science
are blind, but science without the humanities may be vicious.

In stating the case for the humane approach to rhetoric, I hope
I shall not be interpreted as making a plea for a return to the
classics. Classicism is merely an indoctrinated humanism. As
Perry has pointed out, it is no necessary part of humanism. Where
else could the Renaissance have turned for light except to the
Greeks and Romans? The world at that time was a limited world,
and the past a limited past. An additional three hundred years
have gone by and we live in an expanding world, with undreamed
of contacts, necessitating increased attention to the understanding
of the nature of man all over the world. The humane approach
to rhetoric does not mean burying one's self in fourth-century
Athens or first-century Rome. A man is no freer imprisoned in
the fourth century than he is if imprisoned in his own age. The
Renaissance was not humanistic merely because it turned back:
it was humanistic because it searched for a well-spring of creativeness.[38] The real spirit of the humane approach is, I think, in
the words of Kenneth Burke: "Use all that is there to use."[39]

The humane approach to rhetoric and rhetorical discourse can,
I believe, in the words of one of our colleagues, teach us to "love
reason and to value its limitations, to prize emotion but resist
control by it in despite of reason, to cultivate imagination and
cope with its aberrations. . . ."[40] The historian, H. W. C. Davis
has remarked, "Our common humanity is best studied in the most
eminent examples that it has produced of every type of human
excellence."[41] Public address in the great tradition provides us
with many examples of human excellence. Whether one derives
his notion of man, the decision-maker, from the Greeks, or from
the God of the Hebrews, I suspect makes little difference. But
that decision-making be wise, I am sure matters to all of us.

Chapter 11

Rhetoric, Public Address, and History

A few years ago, after I had finished editing the third volume of *A History and Criticism of American Public Address*,[1] I was asked to participate in a symposium with two historians in order to respond to their evaluation of the volume. In a situation like this, when author faces critic, one has the feeling the sinful Puritan might have had when he sometimes called out in despair: What can I do to be saved?

But whatever one's personal feeling, the symposium provides some contemporary presumptive evidence that what the rhetorician is doing may be expected to have some relationship to what the professional historians are doing.

The alliance of history, rhetoric, and public address goes back a very long time. Walter Savage Landor makes Pericles remark: "Show me how great projects were executed, great advantages gained, and great calamities averted. Show me the generals and the statesmen who stood foremost, that I may bend to them in reverence; tell me their names, that I may repeat them to my children . . . place History on her rightful throne, and, at the sides of her, Eloquence and War." Pericles hoped that when the history of Athens from the invasion of Xerxes should be written, it would give "a fair and full criticism on the orations of Antiphon," even at the expense of a narrative of the battle of Salamis.[2]

Helen North, Professor of Classics at Swarthmore College, interestingly points out that rhetoric and history are the two major disciplines, created by the Greeks toward the middle of the fifth century B.C., which have the rare distinction of being foreign to Athens, rhetoric being born in Sicily, history in Ionia, yet which, as soon as they found their way to Athens, near the beginning of the age of Pericles, began to exert powerful reciprocal influence.[3] And the distinguished historiographer James T. Shotwell has spent considerable time in tracing the relationships of the two disciplines, particularly in their early days.[4]

That history was important to the rhetorician and orator is apparent from early statements of the orators. From orator Cicero, we have the word: "To be ignorant of what occurred before you were born is to remain always a child."[5] Knowledge of the past led to political wisdom and was, in ancient times, considered absolutely essential to the deliberative orator and part of his training. Although ancient orators like Atticus believed it to be "the privilege of rhetoricians to exceed the truth of history, that they may have the opportunity of embellishing the fate of their heroes,"[6] nevertheless the usefulness of history to the orator was taken for granted. Examples drawn from history were always thought to be superior for persuasive speeches to those drawn from poetical or mythological lore.

That rhetoric had an influence on history is equally apparent from the dawn of effective historical writing. Most of us know that the early historians used speeches as the substance of history, speeches fairly close to the original model, as in Thucydides' history of *The Peloponnesian War*, or entirely contrived speeches, as in the case of Ephorus, assigned by Isocrates, to preserve the distant past in fitting mould.[7]

North has pointed out that the aims of history writing were in part established by the rhetoricians, and the skills of historical writing were also provided by rhetoricians.[8] It may be added that some of the writing was done by rhetoricians and that rhetoricians judged the results.

The Greek historian, like everyone else, was expected to be a contributor to the virtue of the state; hence, his aims were, at least in part, pedagogical, and his methods didactic.

In the absence of a generalized prose style, or a theory of style for history writing, the historians adapted to the methods and injunctions of the rhetoricians. Theories of narration and of digression were in the tool kits of the rhetoricians, and these readily lent themselves to historical writing. Also, the topics of praise and blame had been carefully worked out by the rhetoricians, and these were useful to the historian in his discussion of the heroes and villains who figured in his narrative. Shotwell, R. C. Jebb, and others, have labeled the period of historical writing between Xenophon and Polybius the "age of the rhetorician."[9] Shotwell has remarked, "The arena of politics was hardly larger than the amphitheatre or the agora, and it was possible to control it almost as definitely by the voice and personality of a speaker." But oratory was not confined to politics. It was an art cultivated for itself, like music today, and people went to hear an oratorical display just as we go to hear a symphony.[10] It was almost inevitable that speechmaking should overrun the narrative of history and play upon the language of historical writing, possibly as inevitable as that the histories of the nineteenth century should be couched so largely in the terms of national politics, or those of the twentieth should include the survey of economics and the sciences. The orations gave to the antique mind the air of reality. Not only in Greek history but also in Roman the narrative was interspersed with long discourses. Caesar, orator as well as soldier, halted the charge to deliver through the mouth of a general some harangue.[11]

Not only did the rhetoricians provide the aims, and some of the substance and methods of early history, but they also tested the results. The sense of the mediocre character of the historical writings of Romans during the Republic is brought out by Cicero in what has been claimed to be the "one treatment of history and its possibilities which has come down to us in Latin literature."[12] In Cicero's *De Oratore* a dialogue takes place between the two great orators, Crassus and Marcus Antonius. Antonius has been saying that no special training is needed by the orator to quote official documents in his speeches—a point with which his interlocutor, Catullus, agrees. "Well, then, to proceed," says Antonius, "what sort of orator, or how great a master of language, do you think it requires to write history?" "If to write it as the Greeks have written, a man of the highest powers," says Catullus; but "if

as our own countrymen, there is no need of an orator; it is sufficient for the writer to tell the truth."[13]

The clue Cicero offers as the reason for the mediocrity of
Roman history suggests that Cicero believed in testing it by the
ideals of eloquence. "It is far from being wonderful," says Antonius, "if history has not yet made a figure in our language; for
none of our countrymen study eloquence, unless that it may be
displayed in causes and in the forum; whereas among the Greeks,
the most eloquent men, wholly unconnected with public pleading, applied themselves as well to other honourable studies as to
writing history; for of Herodotus himself, who first embellished
this kind of writing, we hear that he was never engaged in
pleading; yet his eloquence is so great as to delight me extremely,
as far as I can understand Greek writing."[14] In bringing historical writings to the bar of judgment, Cicero argues, "The sort of
language and character of style to be observed must be regular
and continuous, flowing with a kind of equable smoothness, without the roughness of judicial pleadings, and the sharp-pointed
sentences used at the bar. Concerning all these numerous and
important points, there are no rules . . . to be found in the
treatises of the rhetoricians."[15] And noticing that defect, Cicero
paused to sketch in at least some of the rules by which history
should be tested. The rules, in the main, pertained to style.
Quintilian thought the rhetoricians and orators made the best
writers of history and suggested that when they should retire
from active service they turn their talents to the writing of history, carrying with them the methods of the forum.[16]

Contemporary rhetoricians, I think, tend to look back upon the
good old days when the orator and the rhetorician called the
plays in historical writing and sigh for a return to that position
of respect. But, as Frederick Jackson Turner has remarked, "Each
age writes the history of the past anew with reference to the
conditions uppermost in its own time,"[17] and conditions shift
from century to century and time to time. In 1902, in this country, Josiah P. Quincy, in a speech before the Massachusetts Historical Society, formally proclaimed that oratory no longer dominated history. "It is the widening of the thoughts of men," he
said, "that has caused oratory to diminish its direction of history."[18]

Since its beginning, historical writing has come a long way, and I doubt if anyone seriously would care for a return to its primitive methods, however much the change may alter the position of the rhetorician and the orator. History, like everything else, has been a developing study and has sought to perfect its methods. The little girl in Agatha Christie's *Moving Finger* recognized its variety of forms and its growing pains when she haughtily observed it was "such rot" because it was "quite different out of different books!"[19] It has had its Thucydides and Xenophon, its Polybius and Tacitus; its Von Rankes, Michelets, and Carlyles; its Macaulays and Toynbees; its Croces and Hegels and Turners and Beards. It has had its theories of great men, its men of iron and blood; its spiritual determinism, economic determinism, and social forces; its fortune telling on a grand scale, and its record of God's successive revelations in the universe; its conception of history as an art allied to literature, and its conception of history as a science, related to the natural sciences, or at least to the social sciences.

That the position of rhetoric and public address should change with these various conceptions of history should be no less obvious than that conceptions of rhetoric and public address have varied over the centuries.

Various disciplines have tried to train the historian in his job. Calling on the historian are the economist, the anthropologist, the archaeologist, the psychologist, the sociologist, the statistician, the political scientist, and now the theoretical physicists who, in their study of the electron,[20] find a lesson that may help historians to answer the question that Isaiah Berlin of All Souls College, Oxford, calls the crucial question of our time: Where is the frontier between freedom and causal laws to be determined?[21]

Historians have been asked to deal with economic behavior, political behavior, institutional behavior, military behavior. One is inclined to agree with the pathetic note of James MacGregor Burns that the task is "no job for mere mortals."[22]

Contemporary rhetoricians, too, have been trying to reform the historian. We have complained that historians are not sufficiently aware of the role of oratory in American culture, or any other culture, for that matter, and that they have disregarded or written off the work of rhetoricians in assessing the influence of orators on the flow of history. When Allan Nevins, Columbia University historian, remarked that "poor price tendencies for peasant production may have had more to do with the Crusades than the preaching of Peter the Hermit,"[23] rhetoricians have thought he posed an alternative that historians in the past have not been able to analyze and evaluate. Historians had learned the analytic method and the vocabulary for dealing with economic problems but had not become expert in the analysis and evaluation of rhetorical influences. In the contest between a Georgia Orphanage and Benjamin Franklin's piggy bank, the Georgia Orphanage won out,[24] and rhetoricians have thought the historian quite dense who did not see in this contest the influence of the preaching of George Whitefield. Since historians have remarked that "in nine instances out of ten . . . any important historical transaction should be treated as of multiple causation, its roots as numerous and far-ramifying as its consequences," and that the "office of the historian is not to select one or two explanations, excluding or minimizing all others, but to ascertain *all* the factors and assign to each its proportionate weight,"[25] the rhetorician has sometimes asked: Why don't you practice what you preach? Rhetoricians applauded when Ohio State compilers of the dictionary of political terms pointed out that "in general, while historians like to use the slogans and catchwords of the events they describe in order to add color to their presentations, their treatment of the linguistic side of political activities is very far from systematic and in some cases misleading."[26]

As Carl Becker once wrote about complaints in his own field: "Knowing the limitations of our most famous predecessors gives us all confidence in the value of our own researches: we may not be brilliant, but we can be sound. We have the great advantage of living in more enlightened times: our monographs may never rank with the *Decline and Fall* as literary classics, but they will be based upon sources of information not available to Gibbon, and made impeccable by a scientific method not yet discovered in his day."[27] Many of us, I am sure, tend to believe that historians are missing a magnificent opportunity when they do not make use of our special insights and tools.

I believe that some of our feeling of abuse would be lessened if we as rhetoricians were to turn our investigative and scrutinizing instinct upon ourselves. The good old days have been over for several centuries. In the normal Greco-Roman curriculum, which varied but little from the Hellenistic Age to the age of the Second Sophistic, history had a firm place in the schools, but it was never studied for its own sake—always for what it could bring to oratory. Obviously that position is reversed, and we may well ask with humility: What can the rhetorician bring to history? The answer I should like to suggest is that he will not bring very much of anything unless he conscientiously asks the question: What are the historians doing that may well be supplemented by the work of the rhetoricians? Our first job· is to understand that some of their theories do not admit of any support at all from rhetoricians.

Rhetoricians have been confused at times about what history is and of its changing nature. I am reminded of the charming story of the late Dixon Wecter. A person in a St. Joseph, Missouri audience, after listening to a talk on the centennial of the Hannibal & St. Joe Railroad, in which the speaker described its background of courage and hope as it battled great odds to become an important feeder into the frontier West, came up and told the speaker, "I didn't know that was history. I didn't know the Midwest had a history. I thought history was Plymouth Rock and Bunker Hill."[28] Now, rhetoricians have not been as confused as that, but some have had a grand condescension on what history is, or ought to be. We have enjoyed at the historian's expense the Mr. Dooley observation that "history is a postmortem examination. It tells ye what a country died iv."

Personally, I should like to undertake rhetorical studies that would be useful to the historian if for no other reason than to relieve him of labors which are overwhelming. I do not care to call the strikes. With his overall judgment of the scope of history, I believe he is in a better position than I to say what is useful to him.

I referred at the beginning of this paper to the discussion in which I participated with historians after the appearance of Volume III of the *A History and Criticism of American Public*

Address.[29] I believe the suggestions made by those historians will be useful to all of us who contemplate doing rhetorical studies of orators or movements. The remarks come from kind, generous, and thoughtful men, who were in no sense disparaging of our efforts, one a historian at Syracuse,[30] the other a historian and Dean of the Graduate School of the City College of New York.[31] Their remarks were not off-the-cuff. In fact they were kind enough to prepare them in writing for me, after having spent some four months in an examination of the volume. There are about a half-dozen weaknesses which they find in our critical studies of public address that limit their use to the historian.

First, the historians claim that we do not sufficiently exploit historical and biographical materials, designed to identify the figures we work with as public figures.

Second, they claim that although we struggle with a sense of the times, we do this in no systematic way.

Third, they claim that our tendency is to present the times in isolation and the figure in isolation, without the structure of give-and-take between the two.

Fourth, they argue that we tend to treat the speaker as static by labeling processes that do not make possible the notion of emergence and change.

Fifth, they argue that we tend to define the position of the orator in terms of philosophical beliefs, without showing the figure sufficiently in specific decisions, often having little reference to a basic philosophy.

Sixth, they claim that we have not made an effort to stabilize the criteria for evaluating speeches in different periods and to characterize the oratory of the periods; that we do not ordinarily see beyond the oratory of the particular orator with whom we may be dealing.

Seventh, they argue that we do not show the limitations or extension of our figure by reference to other figures doing the same thing. This would suggest the necessity of comparative studies.

One of the historians, in brief form, set forth three things that the critic of public address could do to aid the historian. I shall quote him:

In brief I want the student of public address to do three things. First, I want a picture of the orator in action. Put his image in my mind's eye and make his words ring in my ears. Place me in his audience and make me hear and see him perform.

Second, while making me into the orator's contemporary, plant in me that same contemporary's listening habits and trained reactions. I want to know why I would consider a speech a success; why I would be persuaded to the speaker's point of view.

Third, I would like to have set forth, in clear language, the standards for judging each era's effective public speaking so that if the rhetorician has not made his evaluation of individual speakers the historian can do it himself.[32]

No serious student of rhetoric and rhetorico-historical writings will believe that these requests are unreasonable. I do not know any historian who is reluctant to accept from allied disciplines whatever enables him to make better judgments and better interpretations. He merely asks that what he uses as historical evidence be examined with caution, systematized, and presented in a language which does not twist and distort. It may be true, as one historian himself has said, that a "few years ago, members of the historical professions seemed much more fascinated by test-tubes and telescopes, millimeters and micrometers, slide rules and comptometers, business charts and statistical formulae, machinery and technology" than they should have been. "While still recognizing the importance of such aids in understanding the affairs of men, the majority of historical scholars appear to understand their limitations as well. That is, historians have come to recognize the fact that, however many persons are affected by technological devices, all such devices are made and must be operated by men. . . . They have learned, too, that however much men may have in common and however important these common characteristics may be, the dynamic quality of society is derived from the individual who sets the mass in motion or determines its direction, and is therefore distinctive."[33] The reigning school of cultural, social, intellectual historians knows that "the molding elements of history include ideas, forces, great men—and chance," and that "a monistic picture of the past which exaggerates the role of any of these four is as unsatisfactory as

an Egyptian painting without perspective."[34] Public address cannot be omitted by the historian. Historians know that one may
safely admit one man's voice has not the power that it had when,
in the agora, it brought whole Greek city states under its control.
But they also know that multitudes who gather regularly to listen
to other men are not all listening with little or no effect on the
cultural web.

What historians were reluctant to do when they were allied
more closely with literature may now be expected to be done as
they strengthen their kinship with the behavioral sciences, for
clearly the behavioral sciences have taken to themselves the study
of verbal behavior. In 1933 Leonard Bloomfeld, a pioneer lin-
guistics scholar, remarked that "psychologists generally treat
language as a side issue" and a survey of one-hundred introductory textbooks in psychology demonstrated that to be a fact, with
only three books giving systematic treatment. Only twenty-five
years later a psychologist remarked in regard to the importance
of language, "anyone who is working on anything else is just
wasting his time."[35]

Although one discovers a bit of belated ecstasy in the remark,
nevertheless, this is hopeful indeed. Make no mistake, not only
psychologists but historians are beginning again to look more
closely to the resources of language.

James MacGregor Burns's biography of Roosevelt handles
with great ability the inaugurals and other addresses of Roosevelt.[36] Richard Hofstadter's book *The Age of Reform*, which concerns itself with the ideas of the Progressives, "their conception
of what was wrong, the changes they sought, and the techniques
they thought desirable" speaks repeatedly of "agrarian rhetoric"
and "the rhetoric of progressivism."[37] Historians like J. G. Ran-
dall, Ralph Gabriel, and Merle Curti show an awareness of the
need for more systematic attention to the ephemeral literature
and to linguistic aspects of public events. The astonishing Chapter 3 on "Exercises in Constitutional Logic" in Kenneth Stampp's
And the War Came is a striking example of the anatomy of the
language of force.[38]

Merle Curti, distinguished Pulitzer Prize-winning historian of
Wisconsin, studying fugitive speeches and essays at Huntington
Library remarks:

Historians of ideas in America have too largely based their conclusions on the study of formal treatises. But formal treatises do not tell the whole story. In fact, they sometimes give a quite false impression, for such writings are only a fraction of the records of intellectual history. For every person who laboriously wrote a systematic treatise, dozens touched the subject in a more or less casual fashion. Sometimes the fugitive essays of relatively obscure writers influenced the systematizers and formal authors quite as much as the works of better-known men. The influence of a thinker does not pass from one major writer to another without frequently being transformed, or dissipated, or compressed in the hands of a whole series of people who responded to the thinker and his ideas. It is reasonably certain, moreover, that in the America of the early nineteenth century ephemeral writings, widely scattered as they were in pamphlets, tracts, and essays, reached a much wider audience and are often more reliable evidence of the climate of opinion than the more familiar works to which historians of ideas have naturally turned. The student of the vitality and modification of ideas may well direct his attention, then, toward out-of-the-way sermons, academic addresses, Fourth of July orations, and casual guides and essays.[39]

How far the historian may be forced to go in making use of analyses coming from language scholars may be suggested by the observation of Herbert Muller: "Historians can more nearly approach the detachment of the physicist when they realize that the historical 'reality' is symbolic, not physical, and that they are giving as well as finding meanings. The important meanings of history are not simply there, lined up, waiting to be discovered."[40] One cannot seriously believe that any historian intends to write the history of modern Germany without reference to the oral barrage of Adolph Hitler, or without reference to the Nazi speaker organizations.[41] Hitler believed that "the power which has always started the greatest religious and political avalanches in history rolling has from time immemorial been the magic power of the spoken word, and that alone."[42] Not many of us would be inclined at the moment to dispute his tragic word. Nor can one seriously believe that the history of modern Russia can be written without reference to its propaganda machine. The number of people at present engaged in trying to penetrate the Russian mind through the fog of its language should give some evidence of the significance of rhetorical study. Every account that I have seen of Fidel Castro's leadership in Cuba has called attention to his spellbinding-power over the masses in Havana Square. Can anyone seriously believe that the modern history of England can be written without recognition of the power Winston Churchill manifested in his speeches; or that the history of modern America can be written without recognition of Franklin Roosevelt's suasiveness? The simple truth is that it is not being done without this recognition, as anyone familiar with recent historical writings can easily discover.

But whereas this is true, I can easily conceive of the history of any country being written without much attention to historico-critical writings produced by many of us rhetoricians.

The historian has had every right to be skeptical about rhetoric and rhetoricians. He is perfectly well aware of the damage that was done to authentic history in the early days when it consisted of contrived speeches. He is also perfectly well aware of the damage done to history by the flowers of rhetoric from the Renaissance through the nineteenth century. The rhetoric which brought popularity to the historian of the third century B.C. just as surely brought neglect of the rhetorician at a later time. Historians are not much impressed with the Ciceronian appraisal of Xenophon's style as being "sweeter than honey."[43] They fear that the rhetorician may be "striving for effect rather than for fact."[44] One must remember that many of them still believe that the rhetorician is mainly concerned with purple patches and with elocution. One of the historians to whom I previously referred described the style of the writings in A History and Criticism of American Public Address as "declamatory,"[45] argumentative assertion advanced vehemently, with assertion counting for more than evidence.

Historians realize that their concern must be not only with the substance of history but also with the recording of it. They readily admit that the mode of presentation is often a neglected part of history. Shotwell remarked years ago, with concern: "Rhetoric and scholarship are by no means irreconcilable, if by rhetoric we mean the use of language appropriate to the occasion." He lamented the fact that "the researcher tends to concentrate upon the facts which he finds in his source material and to have little patience with the restatement of them."[46] Nevins has stated explicitly that the third phase of history is presentation, which involves "that complex and exacting science termed Rhetoric."[47] Historians are aware that a dull narrator "can make even its most meaningful chapters seem drab and unimaginative—an act of exhumation, followed by a grim inventory of the bones." As Wecter has remarked: "The best writing has been defined as the richest thoughts put into the simplest language. As applied to history, such discourse should resemble the easy, informal, but never careless talk of a well-educated man speaking to friends. To bore, to shout, to preach, to patronize, to grow flabbily garrulous, are all bad manners in society,"[48] hence, also bad manners in historical writing.

The simple truth is that historians, skeptical of the practices of rhetoricians, find all too many instances of what they are looking for. When one of our critics, examining the speech of General Douglas MacArthur, on his recall from Korea, announces "the General's address will become an English language classic— even a world classic in oratory,"[49] the historians know such appraisal is declamation, omniscience, Fourth of July oratory. It is neither history nor effective historico-critical writing. What tests of evidence would the historian use to verify such assertion? There is no doubt that our historico-critical writings are often careless, hazy, assertive, declamatory, and sometimes, I fear, self-aggrandizing, rather than "the richest thoughts put into the simplest language."

Historical writing, it has been observed, is contingent upon the general approach to history prevalent at any time. "History, the art, flourishes with the arts," one observer has announced. "It is mainly the creature of imagination and literary style."[50] Macaulay exemplifies this great tradition. On the other hand, history, the science, has a development and a logical history of its own. Impartial, almost inhuman, its concern is not to teach lessons or to be scintillating, but to find the truth and set it forth accurately, and with razor-like precision. Our enthusiasm for our heroes may give verve to style, at times, but that enthusiasm can easily distort the subject we aim to present, and the personality of the author emerges more strongly than the personality of the speaker whose efforts he is aiming to describe. It may be true, as the historian, Theodor Mommsen once said, "History is neither written nor made without love or hate."[51] The historian is inevitably an artist of a kind as he composes his narrative, selecting, shaping, coloring. The greater historians, from Herodotus to Toynbee, have generally been distinguished for their imaginative reach and grasp, sometimes for their special loves and hates, but as Muller has asserted, "not necessarily [for] the soundness of their conclusions."[52] History must always aim at the literal truth, however much an "act of faith"[53] it might be. "A lover of history loves it straight, without chasers of fancy; he is especially irritated by merely picturesque history, or by such bastard offspring as the fictionalized biography."[54] Many rhetorical critics know that they are neither Gibbons, Macaulays, nor Toynbees. We must surely agree with Charles Krey, the distinguished historian, when he says that "in the effort to record and explain the long story of human development, history must continue to seek, wherever it may be found, the language best fitted to convey the thoughts, acts, and feelings of men."[55] The ideal of the great Justice Louis Brandeis for the courts may not be far from the ideal sought in rhetorico-critical writings: "So put it that all your hearers shall not be aware of the medium; so put it that they shall not feel you, yet shall be possessed of what you say."[56]

The ideal of history, says Morris Cohen, is "an imaginative reconstruction of the past which is scientific in its determination and artistic in its formulation."[57] I believe that rhetoricians can implement historical writings in general to the extent that we seek perfection both in our investigation and in our presentation. That day may not be as far afield as it has sometimes seemed.

Archibald MacLeish has observed: "The sickness of our day is the sickness of disordered and multifarious phenomena, undisciplined, unorganized, and uncomposed. Our desperate need is to impose upon the world of chaotic phenomena, an order of understanding."[58] With respect to verbal phenomena, elusive and fleeting, rhetoricians, I believe, are attempting to impose that order. They are not always successful, and work lies ahead. Much work has been too ambitious and hence sometimes superficial. I can recall all too many instances of pride growing out of having presented a 1200-page or a 1400-page dissertation to some graduate school. In our sober moments any of us should know that this is not likely to be all pure gold. Better work is that which Irving Dilliard, a newspaperman, has just done on Learned Hand, carefully selecting and presenting his speeches and making them available to the historian as evidence. The modest job of Robert D. Clark showing "The Influence of the Frontier on American Political Oratory,"[59] or Edward Everett Dale's "The Speech of the Frontier,"[60] set a direction far more sensible than some grander operations designed to show the influence of rhetorical prose on history.

Irving Dilliard's Introduction to *The Spirit of Liberty* is something of a reprimand to the rhetorical critics. "It is a strange circumstance," he said, "that a society that publishes so profligately on such an infinite variety of things has not until now got around to gathering together these eloquent and inspiriting papers and addresses [of Learned Hand]. Even now the pleasant task of assembling them falls to one outside the law, as he has been pointedly reminded at times by certain lawyers and judges. The task goes to an outsider; however, only by default of those many members of the bench and bar, professors of law, professional teachers of philosophy, and others, any one of whom might long ago have so appropriately collected the writings and addresses of Learned Hand for the wide reading they richly deserve. But no one of them has done it. . . ."[61] I would suppose that rhetoricians, whose professional concern is with speeches, might well fall into the category of those "others" that Irving Dilliard talks about.

Quintilian's recommendation that the rhetorician write history is probably not an idle recommendation,[62] but I am sure that we need the added injunction, "Let it be good history." We also need the reminder that the professional historian requires raw materials. These, I believe, may sometimes well be furnished by the rhetorician, carefully selecting and editing speeches, and making them available to the historian. They may also be furnished by the rhetorician doing well-balanced and expertly presented critical studies of orators, comparative studies, and studies which cope with the quality and styles of speaking in various historical periods. By more modest tasks we may indeed make ourselves far more useful than we have sometimes been in the past.

Chapter III

Ghost Writing: Implications for Public Address

I was in England at the time Sir Winston Churchill's fourth volume in his series on English speaking nations, *The Great Democracies*, was published. I remember there had been considerable comment about the amount of assistance he had in writing the book. It became a kind of pastime to sit down with a few people and find parts which sounded like Churchill. Someone would say, "That stuff about battles, that sounds like him; he wouldn't let anybody else write about the battles." Another would say, "That part about relations with America; that is Churchill's prose."

I have never been one who believed that I could detect with unerring certainty the manner of someone else. I have been a little envious of people who have claimed that if they were to find a page of a Robert Ingersoll speech in the Sahara Desert, they would know instantly to whom it belonged. On the other hand, I may have avoided the kind of error that came to one of our rhetorical colleagues in the eighteenth century. Some of you may remember a good Scotsman, Hugh Blair, who preached a doctrine of taste and sensibility. You may also remember that he was fond of the literature of the Highlanders. When a young

lad, James MacPherson, turned up one day with some manu-
scripts, Blair pronounced the fragments authentic fourth-century
Ossian and sent him in search of more fragments. He turned up
with more, since he was ambitious to become a literary figure.
At Edinburgh in 1761, Blair started to lecture on "those characters
of antiquity which the works of Ossian bear," and "to examine
the merits of Ossian's compositions in general, with regard to
description, imagery, and sentiment."[1]

The wise old Sam Johnson, something of a critic himself, was
around and had doubts about the tale of the Gaelic King Fingal
that MacPherson turned up. Fortunately, death spared Blair the
knowledge that his young protégé could concoct epics out of
some fairly unauthentic Ossian.

This is not the earliest instance of ghost writing. It is an instance of a man of good taste indulging in bad judgment, occa-
sioned by the matter of attributing authorship. It illustrates the
problem that confronts modern historians and critics.

Ghost writing seems to be very old. Cicero remarks that
Theodorus was "better versed in the theory than the practice"
of rhetoric and "began to compose orations for others to pronounce." Isocrates "wrote speeches for other people to deliver;
on which account, being often prosecuted for assisting, contrary
to law, to circumvent one or another of the parties in judgment,
he left off composing orations for other people. . . ."[2] "Before
them," says Cicero, "no one spoke by prescribed method, con-
formably to rules of art, though many discoursed very sensibly,
and generally from written notes; but Protagoras took the pains
to compose a number of dissertations, on such leading and general topics as are now called *common places*. Gorgias . . . did
the same, and wrote panegyrics and invectives on every subject;
. . . Antiphon . . . composed several essays of the same spe-
cies,"[3] presumably for others to use.

Turn to Thucydides and the Peloponnesian War and of course
one discovers that Thucydides composed his history from speeches.
Although he tried to be faithful to original models, nevertheless
he composed the speeches that he puts into the mouths of generals and politicians. And whereas he aimed to keep close to the
original models, later historians cut their orations out of whole
cloth.

The ghost has been around for a very long time and has shown up in various places and in various forms. Claude Fuess, headmaster emeritus of Phillips Academy, Andover, Massachusetts, recalls that as a boy in central New York he had to memorize and recite a passage beginning "Sink or swim, live or die, survive or perish, I give my hand and my heart to this vote."[4] One can imagine how some teacher, instilling a message of patriotism, told how John Adams spoke it from the heart in July 1776 at a meeting of the Continental Congress in Philadelphia when some person showed a little reluctance to put his signature to the Declaration of Independence. Perhaps the piece does not lose much when one discovers that Daniel Webster wrote it some fifty years later, and his paper was wet with tears, so much had he projected himself into the earlier Philadelphia scene, when he was aiming at some appropriate words to pronounce in eulogy over John Adams at Faneuil Hall on August 2, 1826. It seems altogether possible to make someone else speak "from the heart."

History is rich in instances of complete or partial assistance in the construction of speeches. Washington had the able assistance of Hamilton and Madison in the "Farewell Address"; Patrick Henry had the able assistance of his first biographer William Wirt,[5] and has no doubt profited ever since, from the skill of an able penman. One wonders when he encounters Henry's rambling speech of opposition to the ratification of the Constitution whether age and subject could account for the difference in diction or whether Wirt's pen was a good bit better than his memory.

Webster himself, although he probably did not need much assistance, profited from the memory of Chauncey Goodrich.[6] About the only thing that many of us remember of the Dartmouth College case, says Fuess, are the lines: "It is, sir, as I have said, a small college—and yet there are those who love it. . . ." The line is not a part of the court proceedings as recorded in Webster's *Works*; Goodrich appears to have conjured up the scene thirty-five years later and described it to Rufus Choate who repeated it for the first time July 27, 1853, in a memorial for Webster.[7]

Historians have long been troubled with the presidential messages of Andrew Johnson. Homer Carey Hockett remarks, "There is good reason for attributing some of them to George Bancroft, so far as the literary form is concerned. Whether they faithfully

reflect Johnson's views is of much more fundamental importance."[8] The same kind of question troubles the historian when
he confronts the problem of authorship of President Jackson's
"Proclamation against Nullification," "the words of which are
those of Edward Livingston, the Secretary of State," and when
he ponders John Quincy Adams's relation to the Monroe Doctrine.[9]

Except for highly literate presidents like Lincoln, Theodore
Roosevelt, and Woodrow Wilson, many of our presidents have
had some kind of assistance; and, as has sometimes been said,
probably the ones who did not might well have profited from a
little turning of phrases. As a matter of fact, even Lincoln may
be said to have had some assistance from Seward in closing his
"First Inaugural."

Not all presidents or public men have looked with favor on
the habit of having someone else "do it," even though they have
found themselves yielding to the practice. The bumptious Teddy
Roosevelt would certainly have had little truck with ghost writers.
Literate himself, Roosevelt thought it was the man in the arena
who counted, "the man whose face is marred by dust and sweat and
blood," who, if he fails, "fails while daring greatly" and alone.[10]
There was President Cleveland who felt "safer alone" and did not
even have a manuscript for his inaugural address, although he
probably had some assistance later.[11] In my own state, there was
the case of Adlai Stevenson who spent about four hours a day
writing speeches during his first campaign for the presidency in
1952 and was slow to yield to the supplications of his staff to
conserve his energy. "I think a candidate should work on his
own speeches," he said, "because that is the best way to acquire
the information and the understanding of the issues of the campaign. It is a learning and synthesizing process."[12]

However, one has to admit that as a public institution, ghost
writing came into its own with seriousness when Franklin D.
Roosevelt gathered a brain trust about him, and since then when
a public speaker speaks, there is always the skeptic around ready
to ask the question: "I wonder who ghosted that one?" Roosevelt
seems to have made a game of it. One can visualize the 7:15 P.M.
scenes in the White House, with Adolph Berle, Benjamin Cohen,
Harry Hopkins, Robert Sherwood, and Samuel Rosenman. Archi-

bald MacLeish and others, of course, dropped in, too. Martinis on about the sixth draft probably would go well as a bracer for the seventh, or for the "reading copy."[13] The lonely operation of a man on March 31, 1917 on the veranda of the White House, with his own typewriter and a bowl of milk and crackers presents a striking contrast. Changes occur with considerable rapidity. Only sixteen years had elapsed from Wilson's lonely composition of the First World War message to Roosevelt's entrance into the White House, but by 1933 Wilson's method of composition must surely have seemed hoary with age.

Since then, of course, Truman had some assistance; and it is common knowledge that around President Eisenhower were Emmett Hughes, Arthur Larson, Kevin McKann, Gabriel Hough, Robert Cutler, and others.

In 1952, the Washington *Post* carried an ad: "Too Busy to Paint? Call on the Ghost Artists. We Paint It—You Sign It. Why Not Give an Exhibition."[14] In 1952 also, the universities got wise and believed that they could offer indispensable assistance. American University had some youngsters "whose dream is to put words into somebody else's mouth. . . ."[15] It is difficult to discover whether or not this romantic desire came of reading Cyrano de Bergerac's lines for Christian, to advance Christian's love affair with Roxane. At any rate, the approximately one hundred-fifty ghost writers who were around Washington at the time were insufficient to meet the demands, and so American University enrolled its first students in ghost writing in February, 1952. I have figured out that if the twenty-five expected enrollees per semester have materialized, there must be an additional four hundred college-bred ghost writers around Washington by now.

Walter Bowman, head of the communications program at the time, labeled the ghost writer as the "indispensable artisan."[16] Eric Sevareid, the distinguished news analyst, had a different word for it when he got news of the course. "A man's own words are a man's own self," he said, as he conjured up a picture of General MacArthur returning from Korea, saying to an aide: "Fix me up a speech for Congress, something about old soldiers never dying."[17] Sevareid wished mightily the professors at American University would talk the whole thing over with Winston Churchill. The course goal, "We'll try to show that you must write so

that your speaker can be himself,"[18] sounded pretty cheap to
Sevareid.

Ghost writers have kept their own score sheets and worked
out their code of fair practices. By 1942, Charles Michelson,
publicity agent for the Democratic party and for the White House
in the early years of the Roosevelt administration, was proud of
the citation by the New York *Sun* that he had "written more
speeches for officials than any one in that field. . . ."[19] And
Michelson himself reports the code the ghosts live by. In his
book, *The Ghost Talks,* he reports the shock he had when, during
one of the presidential campaigns, Stanley High, ex-preacher and
evangelist and a Roosevelt assistant, pranced through Democratic
headquarters at the Biltmore Hotel "proclaiming that he was off
to write a speech for the President—a rather shocking violation
of the rules of the game, as a ghost writer is never supposed to
admit that he is the author of a great man's utterances."[20]

In our time, there is scarcely any public service that does not
use to some extent the "indispensable artisan"—the ghost writer.
A friend of mine once told me what I thought to be a very charming story, illustrating the extensiveness of ghost writers. In the
university, where one may expect considerable literacy, one might
not expect to find the system. Yet my friend was asked to write
two speeches for a college president and, having done so, was
promptly fired. Apparently he was not writing in such a way
"that your speaker can be himself." He presumably was writing
in such a way as to be found out.

Now that the advertising industry has stepped in and will, for
a fee, present you in almost any guise, business is booming. It
presents us with the spectacle of "you name the impression and
we'll find the appropriate symbols for presenting it." You, too,
can be a man in a gray flannel suit. You can either "look with
pride" or "view with alarm" on mere request.

The question must inevitably be raised: What are the implications of ghost writing for the student of rhetoric and public
address? There seem to be two varieties of the artisan, as has
often been pointed out. On the one hand, there is the ghost
writer who supplies the form, that is, in so far as form can be
separated from ideas and content. On the other hand, there is the
assistant who supplies both the form and the ideas, leaving

nothing for the speaker but delivery. I have sometimes thought, for instance, that when a Hollywood star appeared at the Los Angeles National Convention of the Speech Association of America and addressed the association on the virtues of being a teacher, a ghost of the nineties must have been around both in substance and in spirit, and that ghost writing had been brought pretty close to home.

To know what a person is working with is, I suppose, one of the first requisites of a proper understanding and setting of anything. The historian cannot proceed accurately without this, and the critical biographer is also almost helpless without this knowledge. One of the writers in our own field came face to face with the problem of authorship in 1956 when he attempted to work with Lord Brougham. In 1928, one of the biographers of Lord Brougham was working through the maze of unidentified materials in the *Edinburgh Review*. Among the private papers of Brougham was a volume, *Contributions to the Edinburgh Review*, in which Brougham claimed the authorship of five articles bearing on the subject of rhetoric. A biographer, Arthur Aspinwall, argued that "Brougham claimed a great number of articles which were really not his own."[21] Caught up in the maze in 1956, Lloyd Watkins applied every critical method he knew for establishing authenticity, concluding only that the authorship was hard to establish but that Brougham may well be the author of at least most of what he claims. Are all five of the articles Brougham's views on rhetoric, or only three, or perhaps two?

One learns to understand a man through his writing and speaking, and accurate understanding and attribution are imperative and go hand in hand. Can one really understand the mind of James Otis if Otis is approached through the account of the "Writs of Assistance" trial that has come down to us from John Adams, or, on the other hand, is what one is understanding the biases and enthusiasms of John Adams?

Many critics are convinced of the intimate relationship between thought and the language in which it is expressed. A good number of philosophers would argue that the two are inseparable, that the peculiar expression is part of the thought that is being expressed. Hockett, writing about George Washington's "Farewell Address" remarks: "The deeper problem remains whether the Address embodies Washington's ideas and views expressed in the language of another."[22] Perhaps an even deeper problem, however, is whether the modern critic is to interpret the address as an address cleverly shaped by Hamilton into a campaign document for the Federalist party. Did Hamilton's language give substance beyond the intent of the Father of his country?[23] Whose mind is revealed in the address?

The relationship between ideas and words indeed sometimes has devious and far-reaching implications. A rhetorical critic, assessing Arthur Vandenberg's famous bipartisan foreign policy speech of 1945, wrote in 1948 what appeared to be a sensible interpretation: "Vandenberg's espousal of the bipartisan foreign policy arose from a deep conviction that politics should end at the water's edge, and that other nations must have confidence in the consistency of United States foreign policy, regardless of the party in power."[24] Little more than ten years later, Douglass Cater, quoting a leading unidentified journalist on the same subject, reports as follows: "I have had one very important experience in this town. I knew Arthur Vandenberg when I thought he was the most pompous and prejudiced man in the United States Senate. I saw him change partly by the process of mellowing old age, but mainly by accident and particularly as a result of public reaction to his famous speech of January 10, 1945. I happen to know that that speech, or rather the main parts of it, were largely accidental. I can say to you . . . that I was, myself, quite by chance responsible for that change in the speech. But my point is that what changed Vandenberg was not the speech itself, but the press of public reaction to the speech, and from then on, as you know, he played an important role in winning bipartisan support for the concept of collective security." Cater commented, "it was not the first time—nor will it be the last—that the Washington journalist has hailed the policy declaration that he himself had a hand in ghosting."[25] Did the rhetorical critic need to raise the question: How deep was Vandenberg's conviction?

Earnest R. May, Harvard historian, reports in reference to the MacArthur hearings before the Senate Foreign Relations Committee in 1951: "Anyone who has leafed through Secretary Atcheson's testimony will remember how much was made of a speech he had delivered in 1949. Describing the defense perimeter of the U.S., he had apparently deliberately excluded South Korea. When Republicans questioned him about the speech, they wanted to know only two things: had it not invited the North Korean attack; and had it not, in fact, been ghostwritten by pro-Communists in the Foreign Service?" What they sought was "statements admitting guilt either for the war or for tolerating subversion."[26] Thus, the mode of composition of the speech was a target equal to the substance of it, and one might add that in the America of 1951 either was sufficient to destroy a political figure.

There is no gainsaying the fact that for historical understanding correct attribution of authorship is imperative. Unless the origin of thought is ascribed to its originator, accurate assessment of a speech from a rhetorical point of view is difficult, to say the least. The historian Carl Becker has remarked that "you cannot recover the past,"[27] and Charles A. Beard entitled an address to the American Historical Association, "Written History as an Act of Faith."[28] Such statements emphasize the caution with which the critic must proceed in his attempt to be as accurate as possible.

Rhetoricians have always assumed that in judging a speech, the character of the speaker enters into the assessment, his intellectual virtues, his moral virtues, and his goodwill. Now, it appears, since the recent publication of a book called *The Articulates*, edited by John M. Henry and containing an essay called "The Intellectual Gigolo Strikes Back,"[29] that rhetoricians may be all mixed up. It is not the intellect and virtue of a speaker at all that enters into the speech, but the ghost writer expressing himself through the speaker as a "tool." The speaker becomes an oral interpreter of the ghost writer's desire to establish the ghost's connection with the citizenry. "I felt," says the "gigolo," a ghost writer during the presidential campaigns from 1936–56:

> that the candidates really were the expression of me. They were the vehicles by which I expressed my art. . . . Far from feeling inferior to the men whose ideas I assembled for communication to the people of the United States—or jealous of them—I regarded them as a means by which I might communicate, as an individual, to the people. I tried to convey my impressions of and feeling about them as a painter might convey to the public what George Washington or

John Brown looked like to him—or as little Jean Seberg conveys to the public her interpretation of the way Joan of Arc went about France.

. . . I know, many people think of us as fawning, groveling word-workmen, who stand pantingly eager until the Great Man utters a phrase, whereupon we snatch it hysterically and run with it to the public, polishing the gem as we scurry to typewriter or microphone.

As a matter of fact, a major reason the Great Man is great at all is because I, and fellows like me, plus a few thousand political workers, have called him great until the adjective stuck. That's what we work for; that's our job—to make the public think he is great.

Those of us who have worried over the proper attribution of thought expressed in speeches may well be bewildered: ". . . the candidate's thinking is," says the ghost writer, "pretty easy to grasp and write. His thinking is that of the party leaders around him. Otherwise he wouldn't be the candidate. . . . Actually the speech is not his, nor mine, nor that of any other one person," says the writer. "It is the party's."[30]

If there is any grain of truth to the argument of the "intellectual gigolo"—and presumably there is some—one might well ask: What happens to the approach to individual speakers that we as rhetorical critics have superabundantly taken? Orville Hitchcock, reviewing the book for *The Quarterly Journal of Speech*, properly points out that the hero-worship approach to campaign speakers that we have sometimes employed may well be modified.[31] Eric Sevareid's notion that "a man's own words are a man's own self," which has been our assumption, too, in doing rhetorical criticism, takes on an antique air. Many of us had previously found Webster's words meaningful: "True eloquence, indeed, does not consist in speech. It cannot be brought from far. Labor and learning may toil for it, but they will toil in vain. Words and phrases may be marshalled in every way, but they cannot compass it. It must exist in the man, in the subject, and in the occasion."[32] Our critics have worked manfully to discover the uniqueness of the thought of speakers, but it may appear that the labor has been pretty futile. Individuality, according to the gigolo, if it exists at all, is the individuality of the ghost writer, not that of the speaker; but more importantly, individuality has gone out of the speaking situation altogether so far as substance is concerned. The speech represents not the individual but the group. The reality of the character of the speaker passes into the pen of the ghost writer. The speech bears no necessary relation to the thought of anyone. So far as assessing the character of a speaker as an aspect of rhetorical criticism is concerned, the critic appears to be in an almost hopeless position, and we may well ask: "Is rhetorical criticism possible?"

We have long been aware that criticism is crippled in dealing with style. Attributing characteristics of style to a speaker who has a host of ghost writers around him is risky. Think of the spectacle of Hugh Blair making comments on the "characters of antiquity which the works of Ossian bear," and "the merits of Ossian's compositions in general, with regard to description, imagery, and sentiment."[33] Many of our descriptions of the stylistic features of speakers would be simple mockery were we to proceed on the assumption that stylistic features of public addresses represent the habitual language behavior of the speakers we are working with. Anyone could observe that President Eisenhower's ordering of discourse in a press conference bore no relationship to the ordering of discourse and the diction of his public addresses. Newsmen took delight in caricaturing his habitual backing away from ideas, his starting over, his losing his verbs, and sometimes his nouns. Although Earnest R. May's statement to the effect that "ghost writers have built an impenetrable thicket about the truth"[34] may be extreme, there is no denying that a critic of public address can not proceed safely to evaluate the language habits of his speaker unless he knows whose habits of composition he is studying.

It appears that not only should one be aware of the presence of ghost writers doing ordinary work of composing, but we should also be aware of the stylistic tricks that can be played upon a speaker quite deliberately. I have long been aware that when newsmen get miffed at candidates, they tend to pose them in unflattering situations. They can decrease the size of crowds at rallies by a camera angle, and increase them by the same means. They can show the bad side of a profile or the top of a bald head. It appears that the ghost writer can also wreak his vengeance. The next time you encounter "the darndest mouthful of hard-to-handle phrases a would-be official ever tried to put into a microphone"[35] and are totally unable to fit the stylistic features of a discourse into the normal stream of the speaker's talk, you may well, according to the "intellectual gigolo," consider the possibility of the ghost writer's being miffed at the candidate for down-grading him and for not considering him indispensable.

No one doubts, I suppose, that our public officials should not have to spend their energies composing speeches for dedications of ships, openings of canals, unveilings of monuments and bridges, and numerous other occasional affairs. And no one, I think, seriously raises the ethical question involved in ghost writing, since it is taken for granted that a public statement is a public commitment and that an official cannot, in making an unfortunate statement, say, "My ghost writer did it and is responsible for it."

But students of public address may well regret the coming of the ghost writer. Ghost writing, I think, has grave implications for the person who wants to approach the study of public address as humane study. We have long turned to the individual in what we thought to be his great moments of decision, in order to discover in him the marks of humanity. We have looked, at times, to the individual as a guide for our own behavior. But individuality, it appears, is rapidly disappearing. The cry of the contemporary existentialists is that today we are witnessing and are deeply involved in a huge human transformation, a process which goes on silently—the invalidating of the individual. What we have thought to be that most individual thing of all—a man's thought—is giving way to the group mind, or the Flesh formula of speakability, or readability. The student of public address is not putting his eye to the thing that he once was, in the hope of identifying the uniqueness of the creative spirit in public discourse. Claude Fuess is surely right in his observation that a whole fleet of ghost writers could not have coined Churchill's unique way of expressing Anglo-American friendship: "Let it roll. Let it roll on full flood, inexorable, irresistible, benignant, to broader lands and better days."[36] He might have added that a whole fleet of ghost writers could not have said: "With malice toward none, with charity for all, with firmness in the right as God gives us to see the right, let us finish the work we are in, to bind up a nation's wounds, to care for him who shall have borne the battle, and for his widow and his orphans, to do all which may achieve and cherish a just and a lasting peace among ourselves and with all nations." Public address as a humane study has suffered and is suffering as the result of the destruction of human personality, once abundantly present in the great orations. The vibrancy of Teddy Roosevelt, of Lincoln, and Wilson is giving way to a host of unauthentic voices.

That ghost writers can maintain prose on the level that it had been in the past is surely dubious. Ghost writers can doubtless keep the level of prose at least at grammatical accuracy, perhaps even a greater accuracy than was characteristic of some of the great prose of the past. But that a "red pencil" is a substitute for great and impelling prose is not clear at all to me. The critic of public address surveying the body of public prose and finding it at a dead level should not be surprised. Games may be played with language, and occasionally a scintillating phrase, or smart saying may come as the product of joint effort, but that any man surrounded by ghost writers can emerge far and above the level of the group is doubtful.

The truth is that one may search through great bodies of speeches today, only to discover that they could almost have been ground out by an electronic device. The American public scarcely knew at all what to do with a man like Adlai Stevenson in the campaign of 1952, so accustomed had they become to the siren song of the ghosts in political campaigns. So accustomed have we become to the sodden prose of the ghosts, that to speak or write in such a way that individuality appears is to hazard one's political life.

I think there may be another implication of ghost writing for the critic and student of public address. More and more the acts of a public man may be expected to be out of line with the prose that he speaks. I think it true that liberalism is not dead among our public men but a too manifest liberalism in public utterance may well be. Ghosts inevitably must be more conservative, must say nothing that can be interpreted as being extravagantly liberal. Whereas an individual in the past speaking for himself may have been expected to unleash himself at times, his chances for unleashing himself must surely diminish to the extent that he is dependent upon previously prepared and tested utterance.

The student of public address can hardly find a redeeming

feature in the matter of ghost writing. Obviously our work as critics must be more tentative; obviously little can be taken for granted. Perhaps one good thing may eventually come. Some alert student of public address will take upon himself the responsibility of doing a searching study of ghost writing in America. I hope that may be one bright spot in what otherwise appears to be absolute darkness.

Approaches to the Study of Public Address

I have sometimes found myself reading the Preface to that distinguished volume on *British Eloquence* done by Chauncey Goodrich of Yale University in 1852. Some of you may remember how it goes: ". . . in entering on the office of Professor of Rhetoric in Yale College . . . [I] took Demosthenes' Oration for the Crown as a *text-book* in the Senior Class. . . . [My object] was, not only to awaken in the minds of the class that love of genuine eloquence which is the surest pledge of success, but to aid them in catching the spirit of the authors read, and, by analyzing passages selected for the purpose, to initiate the pupil in those higher principles which . . . have always guided the great masters of the art, till he should learn the *unwritten* rules of oratory, which operate by a kind of instinct upon the mind, and are far more important than any that are found in the books."[1]

Chauncey Goodrich felt pretty confident about what he was doing and why he was doing it. I have frequently wished, in teaching a course in American Public Address, that my approach were so well motivated. The assumption which Goodrich takes for granted dates him very well, for the nineteenth century was sure that eloquence led to preferment in public office, eminence in the law, and distinction in the pulpit, and college men were aiming at pre-eminence. What young man, particularly in New England had not looked at the great god Webster and noted both his prosperity and his enormous prestige? It would have been easy enough to attribute much of this enormous prestige to his consummate skill as an orator. With the voice of Webster's ghost still ringing in the ears of the young men of the age, Goodrich could have approached his subject with unmixed confidence that the models of genuine eloquence he presented would somehow serve as a guide to the aspiring men in the front row.

One hundred years lie between Goodrich and the latest controlled experiment on the effectiveness of a speech by Adlai Stevenson, with red lights and green lights flashing in order to record one's immediate response. And I believe that during the hundred years our confidence in what we are about has been shattered. Lord Macaulay could declare: "Parliamentary government is government by speaking. In such a government, the power of speaking is the most highly prized of all the qualities which a politician can possess. . . ."[2] But somehow, at least in this country, after the journalists arrived in the last part of the nineteenth century and the presses started to turn more regularly, other qualities seemed fairly desirable. In our day, with the Madison Avenue men standing ready to meet any emergency posed by an inadequately inspired speaker, and the radio and television announcer ready to interpret the secret thoughts of public men, one wonders whether the power of speaking is highly prized at all.

At any rate, I am not quite sure how to approach the study of public address meaningfully. How should one approach the study of public address in its historical aspects? How should one approach contemporary public address? What meaningful avenues of approach are open? Is there a "useable past" so far as approaches to the study of public address are concerned?

Toward the end of the last century and the beginning of this one, there occurred a rash of collections of speeches such as had not occurred previously and has not occurred since. What did editors hope for as a consequence of presenting multi-volumed collections of oratory? What were their aims and approaches to the subject? Do they offer any light for our time?

Teachers of speech, at the end of the nineteenth century, were not carrying the burden of keeping the art of oratory alive. After Goodrich, the elocutionists had started to dominate in speech education, and their emphasis was not placed on the substance of speaking. So the editors of these collections represented a variety of disciplines. There were Alexander Johnston and James Albert Woodburn, editors, in 1896, of *American Orations: Studies in American Political History*.[3] Johnston was Professor of Jurisprudence and Political Economy at the College of New Jersey, and Woodburn was Professor of American History and Politics at Indiana University. In 1899, came Guy Carlton Lee's *The World's Orators*.[4] Lee was Professor of History at Johns Hopkins University. In the same year, came David Brewer's *The World's Best Orations*.[5] Brewer was Justice of the United States Supreme Court, appointed under President Harrison in 1889. In 1900 came Thomas Reed's *Modern Eloquence*.[6] On the selection committee for the volumes were author Edward Everett Hale, Senator John Gordon and Representative Champ Clark, Atlanta *Constitution* editor, Clark Howell, Professors of Literature, George Harper from Princeton and Lorenzo Sears from Brown. A few other authors and newspapermen completed the list. In 1900, also, appeared *The Christian Herald's* selection of *Masterpieces of American Eloquence*,[7] with poet and social reformer Julia Ward Howe writing the Introduction. Then, in 1902, almost capping the list, came the mammoth *Library of Oratory*,[8] edited by Chauncey M. Depew, Senator from the state of New York.

The prefaces of these volumes give a pretty clear indication of how editors were approaching their task and their subject. I do not know how many persons have gone back to look at those prefaces to find out what the hopes of the authors and editors were in directing the study of American oratory or eloquence, as it was called then. Some of those authors and editors looking at contemporary approaches to the study of public address might well ask: How have the mighty fallen?

Alexander Johnston remarked: "The design which has controlled the present collection has been to make such selections from the great orations of American history as shall show most clearly the spirit and motives which have actuated its leaders, and to connect them by a thread of commentary which shall con-

vey the practical results of the conflicts of opinion revealed in
the selections."[9] Woodburn, his collaborator, writing a Preface
to the revised edition of *American Orations* noted: "As a teacher
of American history, I have found no more luminous texts on our
political history than the speeches of the great men who have
been able, in their discussions of public questions, to place before
us a contemporary record of the history which they themselves
were helping to make. . . . The earnest historical reader will
approach these orations, not with the design of regarding them
merely as specimens of eloquence or as studies in language, but
as indicating the great subjects and occasions of our political
history and the spirit and motives of the great leaders of that
history."[10] In the spirit of Edward Freeman, who thought of history as "past politics," or the "process by which Americans, past
and present, have built and conducted their *state*,"[11] Woodburn
hoped to send his volumes abroad. For him, history was "not
merely eloquent writing, but a serious scientific investigation . . .
not mere anthropology or sociology, but a science of states,"
hence, the study of history was the "study of politics. . . ."[12]
And so Johnston and Woodburn approached the study of oratory
from the point of view of the student of politics, whose concern
was with the rise, organization, and development of the state.
Orators were among the makers of the state.

Although a historian also, Guy Carlton Lee's approach was
quite different. In selecting the orations, says Lee, the "editors
have applied the rule of exclusion. Every oration not a master-
piece of eloquence or an invaluable illustration of a phase of
oratorical development has been omitted."[13] Conceived as a "history of oratory by specialists,"[14] the history is devoted "*to the
living words of the master-orators,* not to disquisitions upon
them,"[15] except for essays devoted to characterizing the style of
the different periods with which the editors deal. Turning for
illustration to the volume devoted to American oratory, one discovers the attempt of the author to present examples illustrating
different periods of development of oratorical style. Thus, "the
Puritan . . . orator was entirely dominated by recollections of
those of England, or by the reports of speeches brought to him
across the intervening seas."[16] Therefore, the orator of the North
was "calm, steadfast, incisive,"[17] while his brethren of the South

were "tempestuous, fervid, enthusiastic."[18] He clove to the "fiery eloquence of the sunny land of France, and modeled upon this his public utterances."[19] As one turns to the sketches of individual orators presented, Otis is "close in his logic and pleasing in his diction";[20] John Dickinson is "almost overprecise in his diction";[21] Patrick Henry is characterized by "enthusiasm," and "the wild sweep of his eloquence carried all before it";[22] Edmund Randolph had a style that "was direct and generally studiously plain, eschewing all of ornateness";[23] and Sam Adams was "close and logical in his reasoning, and his speech was adorned with well-chosen diction and at times with exquisite metaphor."[24]

Lee examined oratory as a literary genre, with the sharpness of the man who knows, discriminating among different styles and characterizing each orator from the point, largely, of his stylistic finesse. He was concerned with the *development* of oratory.

Although Chief Justice Brewer might have been expected to approach his subject with the rigor of the logician, even his advisory council presumably could not keep his exuberance under control, or, it may be, that his council taught him to be exuberant about orations other than those exemplifying the skills of the logician. On his board, he had a member of the British Parliament, two deans of law schools, one professor of history, three professors of romance language, one professor of oriental language, one journalist, one educationist, four college presidents, and an elocutionist.[25] Brewer approached his subject a bit like the literary historian, George Saintsbury. He was a taster of old wines, and he delighted in the variety of wines he tasted. Brewer thought of oratory as the masterful art: "Poetry, painting, music, sculpture, architecture please, thrill, inspire; but oratory rules."[26] He reveled in a fine sort of way in a distinctive art whose end was power and mastery: "Who does not delight in oratory?" he asks. "How we gather to hear even an ordinary speaker! How often is a jury swayed and controlled by the appeals of counsel! Do we not all feel the magic of the power, and when occasionally we are permitted to listen to a great orator how completely we lose ourselves and yield in willing submission to the imperious and impetuous flow of his speech!"[27] Although he saw in the distant future the phonograph and the kinetoscope preserving more of the reality,[28] until that day came, he hoped to present the orators and let their words serve as a kind of photograph of their invisible power. "We may never know all the marvelous power of Demosthenes," he lamented, and "Cicero's silver speech may never reach our ears, and yet who does not love to read. . . . So if on the printed page we may see the living orator, we may look upon his picture—the photograph of his power."[29] Brewer saw in his time the countless books of poetry preserving the gems of poets and feared that oratory might become a "lost art"[30] unless steps were taken to preserve it. So his purpose was "to present the best efforts of the world's greatest orators in all ages,"[31] and where that was not possible, at least to mirror "the style, method, and spirit" of orators, that the great treasures might not be lost.[32] He was frankly concerned with oratory as an art capable of giving "pleasure, interest, and instruction" and published his collection to the end of keeping oratory "an ever-present and increasing power and blessing to the world."[33]

The twentieth century opened with the publication of *Modern Eloquence*. The professor of English is everywhere apparent on the editorial board and in the general philosophy guiding the selections. The editors have endeavored "to preserve for future generations the best spoken thought of the century," that which is "worthy of preserving in lasting form."[34] They have "adhered strictly to the plan of excluding all speeches that cannot properly be classed under the head of oratorical literature."[35] Emphasis on the word *literature* prepares one for the exclusion. Concerned with the oration as literature, they have "for this reason . . . discarded Parliamentary speeches, and all other speeches delivered in the heat of debate, as well as addresses that were found to be fragmentary or unsatisfactory. . . . No address has been included that bears evidence of loose construction and confusion of ideas."[36] The editors have sought to include those addresses which are "characterized by attractiveness of style, clearness and force of thought, and appropriateness of illustration."[37] The editors say, "True eloquence is irresistible. . . . It charms by its images of beauty, it enforces an argument by its vehement simplicity." Orators whose speeches are "full of sound and fury, signifying nothing," only "prevail while truth is not understood, for knowledge and simplicity are the foundation of all true eloquence."[38] "The language of eloquence is founded on thought, emotions, earnestness, humor and enthusiasm. Above all, it requires innate talent, for the secret of verbal magic was never acquired in a school of oratory. In its higher forms eloquence requires natural genius, profound knowledge, a lofty imagination, and an unusual command of the power of language."[39] Noting that this was the "first attempt to preserve unabridged and in lasting form the best occasional oratory of recent times,"[40] the editors sent their volumes out into the world trusting that the ideal of "simplicity and culture"[41] would find a place in "every educational institution and in every public or private library throughout the land."[42] Undoubtedly the best representative of the literary approach to oratory—one might say facetiously that with this last great flourish English departments wiped their hands of oratory as a branch of literature and gave up all effort to separate the wheat from the chaff.

In 1900 also, *The Christian Herald* brought out its *Masterpieces of American Eloquence*, with an Introduction by the poet and reformer, Julia Ward Howe. One may look back askance at the motivation for the volume, particularly in a day when Pat Boone was thought "corny" for singing "The Star Spangled Banner" to the American people on his popular television program. But Julia Ward Howe, addressing the youth of the country with the hope they would be readers of the volume, remarked: ". . . we may well say of these old-time statements of Right and Duty: 'Grapple them to thy hearts with hooks of steel.'"[43] Like the Mother of the Gracchi when asked to show her jewels, America may "point to her true children who have done her work, and borne, with her burdens, a great part of the obligations of civilized humanity: These are my jewels."[44] Julia Ward Howe was convinced that "eloquence does much to build up the life of free peoples. The words uttered by patriots in our early history were prophetic of the destiny of a Nation fated to play a new part in the great drama of the world's record."[45] She saw her day as a time of "fair opportunities of culture and education"[46] and also a time of "lamentable ignorance of the history and original spirit of our Government."[47] "Nothing," she thought, could "bring the people of other times so much within the comprehension of later generations as can the record of what their eminent men were moved to say in the great crises of their public life."[48] Her effort was that of revitalizing the patriotism of the youth of the country. Sam Adams was included, saying, "Truth loves an appeal to the common sense of mankind,"[49] and "he who made all men hath made the truths necessary to human happiness obvious to all."[50] James Otis was there, and Patrick Henry, and Hamilton, and Fisher Ames; and Webster, and Lincoln, and Wendell Phillips. It was the great-hero approach to public address, and it was pointedly undertaken to imbue a spirit of patriotism by presenting the heroic efforts of the past.

In 1902, came the mammoth *Library of Oratory,* edited by Chauncey M. Depew, Senator of New York. Aware that the art of speaking was not then much cultivated, he dedicated the books to "the stimulating interest in this art . . . ,"[51] hoping that readers should find a "never-failing source of inspiration, suggestion and information."[52] "Eloquence is the master element in politics," he thought, "the most interesting and absorbing game that human beings play. It is the universal and beneficent agent of civilization and religion. At the bar, it is the first dependence of the State and the last hope of the accused. Without its graces, no public celebration is complete. For its inspiriting purposes, it places science, statistics, poetry, history and art under contribution."[53] "Real oratory is one of Heaven's gifts which a man may well pray for. . . . There is a personal magnetism about an orator which cannot be defined. It is something in the voice or manner which establishes a connection between the audience and the speaker."[54] He heard much said in his days "to the effect that oratory is no longer effective or useful. But it is the experience of political leaders of all denominations that the orator never had a larger field or could exercise more influence than today. The vast number of newspapers and periodicals which are offered to the public so cheaply have caused a diffuseness of mind. . . . But the speaker has the power—if behind him is a reputation and a character which give force to his utterances—to solidify in the mind of audience—for his cause—this fluid and popular thought. There is no accomplishment which any man can have which will so quickly make for him a career and secure recognition as the ability to speak acceptably."[55]

If I may extend to 1910 this survey of approaches to oratory that occurred at the turn of the century, students in the South may yet remember Joseph Moore McConnell, Professor of History and Political Economy at Davidson College, in North Carolina, whose *Southern Orators: Speeches and Orations,* appeared in 1910. "My chief purpose," he said,

> in preparing this volume has been to interest the young men of the South and the nation in the study of the literary productions and political ideals of our forefathers. Americans have always been great lovers of oratory, but this was true especially of the generations before the Civil War. During that period in our history, most of our great leaders were men of eloquent speech, and an understanding of their lives and speeches is essential to a true conception of our political growth and sentiments. In that day, when newspapers were scarce and the postal service undeveloped, public speakings were the means of educating the people in current questions. The average Southerner, though not so widely read as his brother at the North, was better informed in regard to national political issues. The social organization of his section provided a class who had the leisure to study national affairs and who prided themselves on being able to instruct the common people clearly and forcefully.[56]

Hence, to preserve the literary productions and to revitalize political ideals, McConnell offered Patrick Henry and John Rutledge and Edmund Randolph, Rhett, Calhoun, and Benton, Clay, Stephens, and Breckenridge, Bell, Houston, and Yancey, Wigfall, Davis, Toombs, Benjamin, Hill, and Grady.

When one examines the motives of the editors of oratorical anthologies, he discovers among them approaches to the study of public address which are designed to—

1 Exemplify the substance of statecraft
2 Preserve a literary genre
3 Inspire patriotism
4 Implant ideals, ethical and political
5 Convey information about the growth of the state
6 Excite the imagination to appreciate the efforts of genius
7 Demonstrate the superiority of oratory over poetry and other arts as an instrument of power
8 Unify thought which was endangered by diffusion caused by the spread of journalism
9 Show oratory to be connected with the game of politics
10 Show the development of oratory

11   See oratory as an exercise in magic
12   Present oratory as the photography of power, not form, or face
13   Serve as an instrument of pleasure and delight

One may preserve the substance, if not the diverse spirit, of these particularized aims by seeing in them three general approaches to oratory at the turn of the century:

1   The study of oratory as a literary form with value worth preserving in and of itself.
2   The study of oratory as a historical event through which the traditions and ideals of America are preserved and reinforced.
3   The study of oratory as a pedagogical method for learning the art of public speaking.

In the first quarter of the twentieth century, the charge of keeping the body of oratory alive passed over into the hands of professionals, to us, the teachers of speech. One may be permitted to be heretical enough to wonder at times if the charge has not been so burdensome as to overpower us. Separated from an anchor in history, political science, and jurisprudence, on the one hand, and from the total body of literary lore on the other, the pathway has not always appeared to be without pebbles.

Under the new dispensation in 1910 came Joseph Villiers Denney's *American Public Addresses.* "American speeches have always been studied enthusiastically by Americans," says the editor, "not primarily because of their literary value, but because of their satisfying statement of American ideals."[57] The book "provides a collection of speeches and papers sufficiently extensive to indicate the main line of development." However, says the editor, "the addresses in this volume illustrate the typical varieties of public speech,—the legislative speech of controversial or expository character, the farewell address, the eulogy, the commemorative and the anniversary oration, the debate, the inaugural address. . . ." The material "provided in the introduction and in the notes will indicate clearly," according to the editor, "the direction which, in the opinion of the editor, the study of these American public addresses should take."[58] Clearly, the pedagogue, the specialized teacher, has arrived, and in the Introduction one finds topics on "Occasions for Speaking," "Kinds of Public Address," "The Oral Quality," "Fashions in Public Address," "Methods," and "The Parts of a Discourse" outlined with the rigors of the brief.[59]

In 1922, came *Models of Speech Composition* by Professor J. M. O'Neill, then Professor of Rhetoric and Oratory at the University of Wisconsin. The book was prepared in order to "make available within the covers of a single volume, complete copies of a number of good examples of each of the principal kinds of public speeches common to American life to-day."[60] According to the author, "neither students of public speaking in the schools and colleges, nor busy men of affairs, who are called upon to make speeches on all sorts of occasions, can anywhere find a number of good examples of each of the more common types of speeches without considerable research in rather better libraries than are available to most of them."[61] Thus, public address was to be studied from the point of view of special models and occasions.

In 1928 came *History of American Oratory* by Warren Choate Shaw, Professor of Public Speaking at Knox College. Not written, says the author, "primarily to meet the demands of the general reading public or of special students of American history,"[62] he intended to "meet the long-felt demand for just such a work in the Public Speaking courses of instruction in American schools and colleges."[63] He wanted to "make intelligible to the modern student all the great models of American eloquence that have been handed down to us from the remote, or more immediate, past. . . ."[64] In writing, the author has kept in mind three principal objectives: "(1) to provide the student of public speaking with a vast body of historical information suitable for use in speech-making; (2) to stimulate him, at every turn, to undertake independent research for further interesting and valuable information suitable for use in speech-making; and (3) to give him a course in speech-making, built upon materials contained in, or suggested by, this text, which will develop all his latent powers for strong and original speech-composition and speech-presentation."[65] Not without an eye to the general reader and to students of American history, for "the history of American oratory is the history of the American people, a record of their thoughts, feelings, passions, and ideals," Shaw intended his book nevertheless as a textbook for use in school and college public speaking courses.[66]

In 1930 came *Classified Speech Models* by William Norwood Brigance of Wabash College. "From a tiresome emphasis in the past upon models, 'classical' by tradition and venerable with age," the author admits to have "reacted to the shibboleth of modern speeches only."[67] "There are thousands of 'frozen essays,' reputing to be speeches, entombed in collections of 'Great Orations,'" the editor says. "They must have been very dull speeches. . . . But for this collection special effort has been made to get speeches as they come fresh from the lips of each speaker with all the backlash from the audience included."[68] The editor endeavored "to propound vigorously the doctrine that speeches are not, and never can be, mere essays; that they exist, not on paper, but only in a three-dimensional situation where a man, having a purpose, faces an audience alive with human emotions, and follows through with that give-and-take which we call 'contact.'"[69] "Classification of speeches are of many kinds and arise from many points of view," says the editor. "The one used in this volume is based, not upon the speech *purpose*, but the speech *occasion*. It represents the conviction that this is the simplest and the most practical of classifications; for (1) it compels a careful study by students of each of the general occasions leading to the speech; (2) it allows an analysis of the special problems involved in each of these situations; (3) it stimulates the examination of the various possible speech purposes that may grow out of these situations."[70] In a sense, thus was spelled out the social-history approach to public address, comparable to the literary-history approach to poetry and the fine arts gaining some acceptance at the time. In his pioneer essay on "The Literary Criticism of Oratory," Herbert Wichelns, in 1925, had severed the approach to public address from literature in his observation: "It is not concerned with permanence, nor yet with beauty. It is concerned with effect."[71] Clearly by 1930, for Brigance, the severance was complete, and he involved himself in the question: What is a speech?

In 1943, emerged the first major work of the new dispensation, *A History and Criticism of American Public Address* under the editorship of William Norwood Brigance. With conviction, it announced, "This work deals with the influence of American public address on the flow of history."[72] "Not only is history written with words," it is "made with words. . . . Most of the mighty movements affecting the destiny of the American nation have gathered strength in obscure places from the talk of nameless men, and gained final momentum from leaders who could state in common words the needs and hopes of common people."[73] Although manifestly an attempt to deal with the individual, the figures were seen with reference to the flow of history, and the flow was studded with heroic men who deepened, muddied, or redirected the waters. Oratory was to be approached from the point of view of "effect instead of beauty, . . . influence instead of appeal to the imagination."[74]

Even before the volumes appeared, a suggestion of restlessness had begun to appear. Donald Bryant remarked: "The important work in the history and criticism of American public address now being undertaken in the National Association of Teachers of Speech is a strong reminder that our scholarship is maintaining its confident advance. Even so, the question must ever stand before us: What are we about, and how are we to go about it? If we rest content with established methods and conceptions only, and do not from time to time question our assumptions, we blind ourselves to much useful knowledge and many possibilities of fruitful interpretation." Bryant saw two problems which he thought to be urgent pertaining to our approach to the study of public address: "They may be briefly stated as questions (1) of criticism and interpretation versus historical fact finding or reconstructing the past, and (2) of the individual point of view versus the social."[75] "Probably," concluded Bryant, "it has been the fault of history in the past, and especially the fault of the history of literature and oratory, to let the study of figures obscure or blot out the study of forces and social movements. A corrective balance unquestionably needs to be established."[76] Soon came the study of the public address of movements, represented by such studies as S. Judson Crandell on the Temperance Movement[77] and Leland Griffin on the Anti-Masonic Movement.[78] There appeared also studies representing regions and areas, comparative studies as opposed to studies of individuals.

The restlessness of the thirties and forties continued, manifesting itself in an attempt to relate public address studies to the growing field of intellectual history. From the approach to speeches as forces on the flow of history to the study of speeches as intellectual substance of history may at first appear not a sharp departure. In effect, however, speeches tend to lose their identity as speeches. Nevertheless, by 1947, Ernest Wrage of Northwestern made way for this avenue of approach. "We need," argued Wrage, "to provide a more solid intellectual residual. This may be realized when the focus of a course consists in the ideas communicated, in the ascertainable sources of those ideas, the historical vitality and force of the ideas, and of demonstrable refractions, modifications, or substitutions."[79] "Whether we seek explanations for an overt act of human behavior in the genesis and moral compulsion of an idea, or whether we accept the view that men seek out ideas which promote their interests and justify their activities, the illuminating fact is that in either case the study of ideas provides an index to the history of man's values and goals, his hopes and fears, his aspirations and negations, to what he considers expedient or inapplicable."[80] Wrage argued that "the prevailing approach to the history and criticism of public address appears to consist of a study of individual speakers for their influence upon history. If one may judge from studies available through publication, they fall short of that ambitious goal for reasons which are painfully apparent to anyone who has attempted to assess influence in history."[81] Starting from the intellectual historian, Merle Curti's theory of the "vitality and modification of ideas"[82] or what Max Lerner calls the "naturalistic approach"[83] to the history of ideas, Wrage sought to approach public address from the point of view of intellectual history.

In recent times A. Craig Baird has concerned himself with speeches as a force in American history,[84] and also with serving as a filter for the determination of representative speeches to be permanently preserved. Modeled after Alexander Drummond and Everett L. Hunt's *Persistent Questions in Public Discussion*,[85] in 1924, Harold Harding has approached the study of speeches from the point of view of their provocativeness. Limited to the period from 1946 to 1952, Harding in *The Age of Danger* has been concerned with the "Timeliness and content" of the speeches "rather than literary merit or form. . . ."[86] And in 1954, Professor Wayland M. Parrish and I approached the subject from the point of view of permanence in value.[87]

There are times when one longs for the good old days as he notes the array of choices he may make to the approach to the study of public address. What is true of those of us who are concerned with the speeches of the past is true also of those who are concerned with contemporary public address.

I cannot believe that our approaches represent much gain over approaches of the past. Our concern with models, and forms, our attempt to separate the speech from the essay or poem, our attempts to show the influence of orators or movements on history, our attempts to see the speech in the flow of intellectual ideas, and our occasional approach to public address as exercise in declamation and anecdotal biography may well lack the vitality of approaches of the early part of the century. Doubtless there is also a self-consciousness that robs them of force. Could it be that the turn-of-the-century editors, despite their unscientific and eulogistic historical methods, preserved the vitality of oratory as an artistic form at the same time that they acknowledged it as a direct force in history? If so, can we recapture that vitality while subjecting oratorical events to the more rigorous demands of contemporary historical scholarship?

Our groping may well reflect the influence of a pragmatic philosophy that stems from William James, wherein values are tested by effect. I believe it also reflects the warping of values that comes with specialization. To see a speech in reference to the total web of events requires thorough grounding in history. To see a speech as one of many forms requires an understanding of the historical development of formalized uses of language. When one is faced with the necessity of a thorough knowledge of history on the one hand and a thorough knowledge of the history of oratorical development on the other, he is likely to throw up his hands in despair and settle for some easier way. Narrow specialization is an easier way out. But I doubt very much if we have any alternative to that thorough knowledge of history and that thorough knowledge of the development of artistic form if we are to study public address meaningfully.

The study of public address is not merely an excursion into other fields of learning. It is a matter of finding the relationship to other fields of learning, as one carefully defines his own field of endeavor.

As suggested in an introductory lecture, I believe that the study of public address should be concerned with the free man in his moments of decision, in those moments when he is faced with many alternatives. Great speeches reveal man at the intellectual crossroads of his public life. They are responses to situations that man has had to confront rather than to flee. The study of the ideas and forms that reflect the rhetorical occasion in its full scope and depth requires breadth and comprehensiveness of learning.

A number of years ago, John T. Flanagan, discussing "Three Allied Arts," remarked: "However the study of public utterance is classified, whatever bypaths its partisans choose, it must *ipso facto* include not only an analysis of speaking itself but a study of the climate which produces it and the aesthetic qualities which it possesses. In this way, history, literature, and public address coalesce, a triad which grows sturdier when the claims of each member are recognized."[88]

Chapter v

Theory and Practice of Rhetorical Criticism

In Athens, after the great Periclean age, the comic dramatists had some saucy things to say about literature. Aristophanes, especially, was saucy, and his chief literary target was the tragic dramatist Euripides. The earliest piece of extended literary criticism which survives from classical antiquity is a debate in the *Frogs* of Aristophanes, about 405 B.C. Dionysus, patron and god of the theater festivals, has descended into Hades to bring back to earth the modernist Euripides, but in the end actually makes an award to the old-fashioned writer Aeschylus. The announced standards of criticism are "skill in the art" and "wise counsel for the state." The actual decision of Dionysus seems to rest not so much on an appeal to either standard as on the fact that Aeschylus is the poet of his "soul's desire." Aristophanes criticizes the "wild and whirling magniloquence" of Aeschylus, with his "hippalectors" and "tragelaphs," and the sentimental fondness of Euripides for lame beggars as heroes. The thing that a critically inclined person may remember most vividly, says William Wimsatt, literary critic at Yale, is a certain directness in the confrontation of the critical object. Scales are brought out, and the poets are weighted against each other line for line:

DIONYSUS: Now, then, each repeat a verse.
EURIPIDES: "I wish that Argo with her woven wings,"
AESCHYLUS: "O streams of Spercheius, and ye pastured plains."
DIONYSUS: Let go! See now—this scale outweighs that other.
               Very considerably.[1]

Although this is a parody of critical procedure, taken from drama, one may respond to it as a symbol of something that is very refreshing in early critical comment. There is a certain frontal naïveté, an immediate shrewdness of inquiry, that is obscured in modern critical formulations.[2] The scene suggests also that however sophisticated the formulation, in the long run, something besides proclaimed ideals may enter into the final judgment.

The critical parody may suggest that literary and rhetorical criticism did not begin in our time, although in moments of enthusiasm some of us may act as if we created the whole idea. If one looks into ancient rhetorical writings, he finds Aristotle commenting freely on the virtues and defects of his contemporaries, and Cicero saying of Cato "good gods! what a wonderful man! I say nothing of his merit as a citizen, a senator, and a general; we must confine our attention to the orator. Who, then, has displayed more dignity as a panegyrist? more severity as an accuser?—greater acuteness of sentiments? or greater address in relating and informing."[3]

Critical practice has been continuous. Centuries, like the eighteenth, and the early part of the twentieth, have sometimes been referred to as "ages of criticism." Surveying the critical practice of rhetoricians and others in nineteenth-century America, Barnet Baskerville found a great deal of commentary, even though he did not find it to be particularly systematic.[4]

In our own times, at least by 1925, rhetorical critics began to find their way. Herbert Wichelns' "Literary Criticism of Oratory"[5] in that year undoubtedly has had something to do with giving impetus to a more systematic approach to criticism and to what might be considered something of a critical movement among rhetoricians. A. Craig Baird and Lester Thonssen's *Speech Criticism*[6] came along eventually, and, of course, the three volumes labeled, *A History and Criticism of American Public Address*.[7] This is to say nothing of the scores of critical studies that have appeared in *The Quarterly Journal of Speech,* and *Speech Monographs,* and in unsung masters theses and doctoral dissertations.

To use the biblical expression, we have among us a great number of people who are "judges and dividers." Most of us do not, like the judicious Plutarch, writing of Demosthenes and Cicero, disclaim responsibility "to criticize their orations one against the other, to show which of the two was the more charming or the more powerful speaker."[8]

When we as rhetoricians get hold of a speech, particularly those speeches that have come down to us from the past, we sometimes forget that the critical process is already well advanced, not rhetorically perhaps, but pretty well advanced, nevertheless. Consider for a moment what has happened to make a body of materials available to us. Usually only those speeches that have endured certain preliminary tests reach us at all. Sometimes an event made the preservation of the speech worthwhile to someone. Sometimes the historian has seen fit to preserve materials that would serve as documents for his writings. Sometimes the price of printing has discouraged a speaker from keeping his speech in print, or the wealth of another has made a speech readily accessible. Sometimes contemporaries have commented so freely on a speech that they made at least parts of speeches available, as for instance, John Adams on James Otis' "Writs of Assistance." Patriotism has sometimes entered in, as in the case of the preservation of the address of General MacArthur to Congress after being relieved of his command in Korea. Teachers have preserved speeches or parts of them as pedagogic devices for teaching fine writing or fine expression. Old copybooks have preserved bits of old speeches on which to base writing exercises. McGuffey readers instilled patriotism in the young through appropriate speeches. Then, there is the matter of language. Most speeches one works with have had a better chance of survival because they were in a tongue we could understand. Finally, speeches get to rhetoricians who claim to approach them with their unique yardstick.

With so much critical operation preceding us, one might ask: Why, more? And I suppose it behooves all of us to ask at times: What are we doing? What is our nature as critics of speeches?

Does what we do have any validity or utility? Do we do well what we are doing? Should we also join the skeptics among the literary critics and ask the question: Is rhetorical criticism possible?[9]

A number of years ago, Loren Reid of the University of Missouri had considerable doubt about the state of rhetorical criticism. Observing what he thought to be some of the misguided notions among our younger critics he warned: "*Rhetorical criticism is not simply a discussion of the speaker's ideas*"; it is "*not simply a classification or tabulation of rhetorical devices*"; and finally, it "*is not primarily an excursion into other fields of learning.*"[10] He made these observations on the basis of the criticism of the habits of some of our younger critics learning their trade. He was not primarily concerned with the slender body of critical lore presented by our most mature critics, who, if not exhibiting the same tendencies, exhibit other tendencies which may not provide a clear line of approach for younger critics to emulate.

You will recall that a few years ago a few of our most mature critics applied themselves to critical examination of the same speech.[11] It was the speech given by General Douglas MacArthur, at the time of his recall from Korea by President Truman. Most of the critics had at one time or another committed themselves to an Aristotelian theory of rhetoric, that is, a consideration of rhetoric as a discovery of all the available means of persuasion. In spite of theoretical commitment, in actual critical practice, there seemed to be considerable disregard of Aristotelian principles. Professor Karl Wallace in examining the critical comments of the critics, discovered with some amazement, no doubt, that "the professional critics of public address" paid "little attention to appropriateness of idea, issues, and arguments." They did not deal "fully" with the invention process, traditionally assumed to be the most important part of rhetoric. Some of the critics reflected "confusion implicity in some of the traditional rhetorical categories." He found in the examples of criticism before him that the treatment of form, when "mentioned at all," was "almost casual," judgments being "unsupported and undeveloped," and "at times even ambiguous and conflicting."[12] In truth, another critic sizing up the same set of critical comments found at least two critics diametrically opposed on all of the major critical categories and, also, that they involved themselves in mutual contradictions.[13] A historian examining the third volume of *A History and Criticism of American Public Address* commented not long ago that it was obvious even to the historian, not primarily concerned with rhetorical criticism, that our critics do not see "eye to eye"[14] on critical theory, therefore could not be expected to reflect much harmony in critical practice.

We have sometimes argued that differences and variation are good for us, and I believe that to be true, but I am not sure that differences stemming from wholly different conceptions of the nature of rhetoric can be good for us or for anyone else. If we are not sure what we are looking for, doubtless we are not going to find much that is significant. Underlying all Loren Reid's complaints is the problem of defining our intent. Take, for example, the difference in conception of rhetoric involved in the two following observations, each having been made by colleagues and acquaintances: The first, "his arguments were specious but his rhetoric was good." Or, take another, "if I had to examine style, I would leave the field."

In these two instances, what one observer does not get rid of, the other one does, and there would be a real question about what would be left. If rhetoric were to be separated from both argument and style, doubtless there would be little left. Presumably we are dealing with a verbal art, and it would be hard to talk about a verbal art unless one had something to say either about the conceptive content of it or the form of it.

These different points of view are traditional, and one finds them embedded in such commentary as that which comes, on the one hand, from the literary historian, Vernon Louis Parrington, and on the other, from an editor of Lincoln's speeches, Roy Basler. Parrington remarks of Lincoln: "Matter he judged to be of greater significance than manner. Few men who have risen to enduring eloquence have been so little indebted to rhetoric. Very likely his plainness of style was the result of deliberate restraint, in keeping with the simplicity of his nature."[15] On the other hand, Basler comments: "It would be difficult to find in all history a precise instance in which rhetoric played a more important role in human destiny than it did in Lincoln's speeches of 1858."[16]

Much of our difficulty comes, I think, from failing to reconcile
two fundamentally different traditional conceptions of rhetoric,
the Ciceronian tradition and the Renaissance tradition. The one
argued that rhetoric concerned itself with five canons—invention, arrangement, style, memory, and delivery; the other, stemming from Peter Ramus argued that rhetoric was essentially a
matter of style and that invention and arrangement were parts
of logic. In our day, matters are not simpler, for traditional conflicts are complicated by notions stemming from popular usage
on the one hand and from scientific procedure on the other.

One wonders at times with I. A. Richards if the word rhetoric
can really be salvaged or if such confusion results from the word
that efforts of clarification are useless.[17]

Many of our theorists seem to accept the ancient tradition,
as interpreted by Charles S. Baldwin, that the business of the
rhetorician is the "energizing of knowledge and the humanizing
of truth."[18] However, in practice, our critics sometimes forget
the knowledge that is being energized or the truth that is being
humanized.

It was very peculiar indeed that, not the professional rhetorical critics, but the journalists examining MacArthur's speech
concerned themselves seriously with the truth of MacArthur's
assertions, the accurate sizing up of conditions in Asia. With a
certain frontal attack, uncomplicated by the study of rhetorical
theory, they commented on the truth of the assertions. When
men listen to speeches they are not unconcerned with the truth
of statements made. I agree with Richard Weaver who remarks:
"There is no honest rhetoric without a preceding dialectic,"[19] that
is, without concern for the discovery of truth. And the remarks
of Baskerville are well taken: ". . . today's critic often side-steps
inquiry into the basic soundness of the speaker's position, offer-
ing the excuse that truth is relative, that everyone is entitled to
his own opinion, and that the rhetorical critic's task is to describe and evaluate the orator's skill in his craft and not to become
entangled in complex ethical considerations."[20]

Is there a significant approach to rhetorical criticism other
than one which concerns itself with the assessment of the truth
and relevance of statements? "In the end," says Baird, "we students of speech are concerned with the recognition of truth and

the speaker's relation to attitudes and movements that support truth."[21] I believe that the critic who fails to face up to the matter is merely marking time or participating in exercises. He is making no fundamental contribution to a better life.

Often we substitute an analytic jargon for analysis. A friend of mine collected a number of comments taken from rhetorical studies done on Adlai Stevenson and sent them to Stevenson. They included such commentary as: "Stevenson employs examples based on historical and invented parallels, demonstrative and refutative enthymemes, and maxims," and "Stevenson's style is middle, neither plain nor grand, and is characterized by perspicuity, adornment and wit. His wit consists of anecdotes, satire, and the bon mot. His bon mots are artistic, for they are based on partial maxims and disjointed enthymemes." Stevenson conscientiously read the critical comment and "roared" because, as he said, "I didn't understand a word." I have just been reading a recent book. In a passage on speeches, the comment goes like this: "The manuscript of an address may be referred to, frequently, as an address. Here, also, a further distinction is necessary. A writer can employ the form of an address and produce a work of literary stature, yet this work may be neither suitable for delivery nor intended for such delivery. A work of this sort is not truly public address; it is not composed for delivery in public, but for the reader in the privacy of his home. In the vocabulary of public address, there seems to be no term suitable to describe this form; we can, therefore, borrow a term from the theatre and label this *closet address*." I confess I do not understand a word. "We can define the speech, then," says the same writer, "as a form of communication in language suitable for delivery by a speaker before an audience, and seemingly so intended, for the purpose of affecting the thoughts, feelings, and, at times, actions of that audience. If the style of the language and the significance of the purpose give such a speech literary stature, we have an *address*."

I have often noted in doctoral examinations, as some of you have, that representatives from other departments often look quite mystified. There is a self-consciousness about our jargon that sometimes makes comprehension impossible. But worst of all, there is a substitution of ritual for the main business.

It may well be that our critics have not settled on a fundamental purpose for doing critical studies. So often when one
works on speeches of the past, he feels no sense of urgency. In
the main, he may be participating in exercises for his own aston-
ishment or amusement. I have rarely discovered in our critical
essays the sense of purpose that is to be found in Kenneth Burke's
analysis of Hitler's *Mein Kampf*. I want, says Burke, "to discover
what kind of 'medicine' this medicine-man has concocted, that we
may know, with greater accuracy, exactly what to guard against,
if we are to forestall the concocting of similar medicine in America."[22] There is no shying away from the responsibility of getting
at the bottom of things here. When one is confronted at the outset with the appellations of "medicine-man" and "concoction" he
is aware that a judgment has been made, a moral judgment, and
that discourse is being treated as if truth had some relevance to
the destiny of a people.

But the destiny of a people is not only a matter of the truth of
statements; it is also a matter of the fitness of things. The critic
who remarks that "if I had to examine style, I should leave the
field," forgets that the critic is responsible, in part at least, for
maintaining a level of language that is in some way harmonious
with the level of development that we presumably have achieved.
Certainly the critic must share the responsibility for the decline
of language that one notes all around. As Wallace pointed out
in reference to our mature critics, if they dealt with form at all,
they dealt with it in a most casual way.

To the question: What is Art? the Italian philosopher, Croce,
once jestingly replied, "Art is what everyone knows it to be."[23]
This same intuitive position might be taken on the question:
What is form? I am not using the notion of form in any highly
idealistic sense, like Plato's "forms of the mind," or even Aristotle's concept of form. I am simply using the notion of form to
pertain to the structure of discourse and the tactics of style.
Emerson would have called it that "power to fix the momentary
eminency of an object."[24]

Studies that have had primary concern with a recognition of
formal devices of language have not been numerous, in comparison with the so-called figure study and the movement study,
which often give only the scantest attention to style, if any. We

have seen a brief flirtation with the study of rhythm in oratorical prose, genetic approaches to style, studies in the differences between written and oral style (both quantitative and qualitative), studies in "loaded words," propaganda techniques, and symbol analysis. The flirtation seems never to have developed into an abiding love of any sort, and sometimes we appear to give up the pursuit as fruitless. Perhaps we have found wanting our critical approaches to language and style and have not searched seriously for more fruitful methods of analysis.

Alfred North Whitehead has commented that style is "an aesthetic sense, based on admiration for the direct attainment of a foreseen end, simply and without waste. Style in art, style in literature, style in science, style in logic, style in practical execution, have fundamentally the same aesthetic qualities, namely, attainment and restraint. . . . Style, in its finest sense, is the last acquirement of the educated mind; it is also the most useful."[25] If style is "useful" as Whitehead suggests, rhetorical critics have given less attention to it than it deserves. I do not mean that biographical, and regional, and movement studies should exclude all commentary except that pertaining to the style of the speakers, but I do mean that critics cannot shirk attention to language, as they have done in the past. Just as literary critics have been forced to agree that in the last analysis attention must be focused on the art object if one is to evaluate it, so we may conclude that closer examination of the language of the human being in his moment of decision must be one of the means to our end. If rhetoricians are dealing with an art—and some of us tend to think we are—then the question is: How does creativeness manifest itself in the speech? the particular speech? How does it manifest itself in structure, in diction, in sentence movement? If the artist is the "maker" as Aristotle would have us believe, what is the form of that which is made, since form is presumably the essence of art?

The London *Observer*, commenting on the speeches of Adlai Stevenson, remarked: "Like Churchill he uses word constructions and images which all but a very deft and courageous speaker would fear to be above the heads of their audiences, but which, in fact, people will willingly reach up to, and applaud themselves for doing so."[26] We may well devote some time to the question:

What is the nature of the word constructions and images that show deftness? What do these structures do for a listening audience?

Woodrow Wilson remarked: ". . . clearness, force, and beauty of style are absolutely necessary to one who would draw men to his way of thinking; nay, to any one who would induce the great mass of mankind to give so much as passing heed to what he has to say."[27] And of Adam Smith, Wilson remarked: "He was a great thinker,—and that was much; but he also made men recognize him as a great thinker, because he was a great master of style—which was more."[28]

We are in a period of great confusion in regard to the nature and function of language and style. We are enjoined on the one hand by a modern linguist to "leave your language alone."[29] "The merit of what a person says . . . is not affected in any way by the way in which . . . [he says] it."[30] A textbook writer tells us "don't worry too much about the exact meaning of words. . . . In a speech those exact meanings may be lost entirely."[31] The same author in telling how to build a unit of a speech, remarks: "Yes, quote Socrates, Plato, Marcus Aurelius, Cato, Homer—any known person who lived long ago. Few in the audience will know the quotation you select, so you can change it a bit to prove your point."[32] On the other hand, a distinguished modern philosopher remarks: "At the point of the abstract ultimate what is said . . . and the way it is said . . . may be the same thing."[33]

After searching carefully in the critical writings of many of us, Helen Schrader came to the conclusion that "not only are contemporary critics of rhetorical style unable to distinguish oral from written style, and what the orator did from their impressions of what was done, but they are also confused as to the nature of style itself."[34] "Their statements are often based on untenable assumptions, and their conclusions are even contradictory."[35]

Close scrutiny of language may yield us better than we know. In his *The Language of Politics*, Harold Lasswell made the statement I wish a rhetorician had made. He remarked with some impatience that "the main incentive for studying the speeches of Wilson, Roosevelt or other orators has been to learn more about the technique of effective discourse." That, I think is an accurate description of what we have been doing. However, he goes on to say, "No doubt, this will continue to be the most patiently cultivated part of the field of research on communication." Then he adds,

> In the long run, however, the study of style may make its largest contribution in relation to the problem of interpreting significant political trends. Certain changes in style may indicate the gradual decline of democratic feeling, or reveal the ground swell of gathering crisis. Style characteristics may prove to be diagnostic criteria for the disclosure of destructive or creative political personalities. For style is not to be dismissed as ornamentation. The most important thing to be said about style is that it can not be exhausted, since style is an indispensable feature of every configuration of meaning in any process of communication. The analysis of what is communicated—of content—calls for the examination of purport and style.[36]

There is no hint here that studies in stylistics are barren or profitless.

Traditionally there have been several reasons for the study of style: we have studied it at times to learn about the personality of the speaker; we have studied it to learn something about the spirit and sense of the times; we have studied it for pedagogic reasons; we have studied it as an aesthetic exercise. It becomes apparent that we may study it for additional reasons. We may study it for diagnostic reasons, and for learning about social tensions. Perhaps we could also study it among our speech deviates in order to learn what differences exist between the normal patterns of expression and the patterns which deviate from the normal. But certainly we should study it to help prevent the decline in language usage apparent everywhere.

The opening lines in George A. Miller's book *Language and Communication* go like this: "Since few courses in language and communication are currently offered in departments of psychology, a few words of advice may prove helpful to psychologists who contemplate introducing such a course."[37] It is a literal fact that some of the psychologists believe that they are about to meet a need which is fulfilled nowhere at present. Our critical studies indicate that we are uncertain about dealing with the matter. It seems ironically true that teachers and critics who, in the nineteenth century seemed to think that the center of rhetorical comment lay in style and language, in the twentieth have so neglected this phase of analysis and criticism that some one believes the field is wide open to "newcomers." There are many newcomers, we have been told, pre-empting the field, which for two thousand years has been distinctively that of the rhetorician: the psychologists, the anthropologists, the psychoanalysts, the semanticists. This is an area in which rhetorical critics should be expected to make a distinctive contribution, and to lead the way rather than follow the way. Donald Bryant has correctly concluded, "Style must not, it cannot usurp the principal place in the attention of the rhetorical critic, but it deserves a place only less than co-ordinate with invention, of which it accomplishes the ultimate fruition."[38]

It is not merely that we need to look to the style of the orator we evaluate. We need, desperately, the right language to report our critical insights. Who can give the sense of the drama of an occasion with a vocabulary so lifeless that it can convey little except the pedestrianism of the critic's mind? Who can convey accurately the facts of a situation without a language flexible enough to make fine discriminations? Who can report on the logic of a case without a language that is capable of precision and exactness in stating relations? Language can be an instrument for conveying truth only if it is used adequately; it can convey a sense of drama only if it is used with sensitivity and imagination; it can be used to discuss style, only if the critic has a sense of fitness.

For a long time editors of our national journals have complained at the quality of the writing represented in them. We need not look to educationist prose, or government prose, as John Ciardi has suggested, for instances of the decline of language usage.[39] We find it in our own journals. So accustomed are we to having the ability to rise on any occasion to say a few words, that we sometimes do not take the time to see what the words are saying. It has been said that "statistical truth is no truer truth than linguistic truth." There are times any editor may think so when he is looking at a manuscript whose truth, if there is a truth, is difficult to discover. I shall always recall a review in an English journal in reference to a critical piece by an American rhetorician. The comment was: How can anyone write like this in the land of Abraham Lincoln?

The late Ross Scanlan has superbly dealt with the Nazi rhetoricians in his two fine articles that have appeared in our journals. One of the interesting discoveries that he made was that the Nazi speaker was advised to study the German classics. "The speaker—not only the beginner but the expert—must continuously study the best works of our greatest poets. In this way he will amass a large treasury of words, and the best forms of expression and beyond that, a steadily widening sphere of knowledge." The speaker must have a "knowledge of belles lettres, especially a detailed acquaintance with the classic German writers—Goethe, Schiller, Gillparzer—and also philosophers like Fichte and Schleiermacher." Only those who knew the sufferings of a people will know "how to coin expressions that are right for the people."[40]

No one wants our critics to imitate the message or the methods of the Nazis. But there is one thing that even that degraded culture suggested, that is, the right expression counts for something. It is necessary to the critic who is investigating the meanings of an orator, and it is also necessary to him in reporting the results of his critical insights. It is important that our language suffer no further decline. Cicero's advice to the orator was "let him have a tincture of learning; let him have heard and read something."[41] That advice is imperative for the critic as well. Our duty as critics may well be to help supervise the language of our culture and to warn ourselves and others when our language is ceasing to advance the ends proper to men. "We infer the spirit of the nation in great measure from the language," remarked Emerson, "which is a sort of monument to which each forcible individual in a course of many hundred years has contributed a stone. And, universally, a good example of this social force is the veracity of language, which cannot be debauched. In any controversy concerning morals, an appeal may be made with safety to the sentiments which the language of the people expresses. Proverbs, words, and grammar-inflections convey the public sense with more purity and precision than the wisest individual."[42]

Rhetorical criticism for our time is still the same as rhetorical criticism in 405 B.C. We are once again confronted with the

Dionysus of Aristophanes announcing his standards of criticism: "skill in the art" and "wise counsel for the state." Our topical concern may be with "style" and "content," or "language" and "truth," but the function of the rhetorical critic remains the same. He must serve his society and himself by revealing and evaluating the public speaker's interpretation of the world around him and the peculiar means of expressing that interpretation to his generation.

Kenneth Burke:
Rhetorical
and
Critical Theory

Whenhen Loren Reid pondered the titles of certain articles—
"Kenneth Burke and the 'New Rhetoric,'"[1] and "I. A. Richards
and the 'New Rhetoric'"[2]—he made the remark that the author
should be thought of as the John Gunther of rhetoric, having gone
inside Burke and inside Richards, in about the way Gunther went
Inside Asia, and *Inside USA*. He may have thought the similarity
stopped there, that whereas Gunther came out again, I stayed
inside. It probably looks as if I am an antiquarian at heart, with
a penchant for modern materials.

In indulging my antiquarian penchant, it is not for the purpose
of staying inside either Burke or Richards. Doubtless rhetoricians
will be unable to sustain much longer some of their rituals and
it is time to look about for light anywhere it may be found. One
discovers that what light is shed by either of the two men in
question comes from entirely different lenses, the one from empirical, even positivistic science, the other from philosophy. I see
men like Burke and Richards as provocative men who provide
a stimulus and who may give promise of providing rhetoricians
with a theory which is better adapted to the learning and thought
of modern times than any conception arrived at two thousand

years ago for a culture quite different from our own. One may as well admit that the word *rhetoric,* as used currently, does not call up common meanings.

Sometimes it is said that the creative writer of the past on sending out his writing could take for granted a relatively stable set of meanings. The writer could assume that if he happened to say a man got a splinter in his finger, readers would take it to mean just that. Nowadays, a mention of a splinter may well be taken as a symbol for a shaving from the true cross.[3]

Doubtless the ancients, in a closed world, listening to hundreds of speeches in a context of common knowledge, could talk understandably to each other, using *rhetoric* as a common term with confidence and precision. I doubt if our knowledge has brought much stability to our meanings.

Someone once remarked that many men start off in life by building mansions in the sky and end up by building a chicken coop in their back yard. The man I want to discuss would admit to having started off in a quandary. In the last few years, he has gone on to draft the structure for a whole new educational mansion.[4]

A good many people would classify Kenneth Burke as the most perceptive critic now writing in America.[5] Among them would be W. H. Auden and Charles Morris,[6] with whose interest in language you are probably familiar. Many literary men find him the "headiest" of the lot.

It would not be misleading to say that Burke has reached his present stature through singular devotion to a study of man and his language-using habits. This study apparently began sometime in the 1920's, was revealed in a little book called *Counter-Statement* in 1931, and was well launched in his first major work in 1935, *Permanence and Change.* With the word "communication" now fairly well established as a household word, one finds it a little hard to believe that in 1935, when Burke proposed to call a book *Treatise on Communication,* the publishers assured him that the title would suggest a book on telephone wires. So Burke was persuaded to accept the title *Permanence and Change.* Since 1935, his interest in language has continued and has manifested itself in *Attitudes Toward History, A Philosophy of Literary Form, A Grammar of Motives,* and *A Rhetoric of Motives.*

Presently, he is at work on a book to be entitled *A Symbolic of Motives.*[7] So definitely is he launched that the doctoral candidate has already got hold of him. If nothing else, he will at least be embalmed in the crypts of the dissertation sections of university libraries.

I had assumed that since 1935 I too had something to do with communication, but the first of Burke's books, encountered some ten years later set me to wondering. I suppose all of us get accustomed to look at what we are doing in a certain way and after a while have a kind of "trained incapacity" for looking at things in any other way. The truth seems to be that among other reasons for what appears to be almost insurmountable difficulty in understanding Burke's works is our own intrenched habit of looking at things in a different way. We are a bit like chickens that can be conditioned to respond to a bell as a food signal, but will respond to the same bell as food signal at a time when the bell means that one is to be led off to slaughter.

I want to deal with Burke's ideas from five points of view:

1   The bases of communication
2   The essence of rhetoric
3   The scope of rhetoric
4   The method of accomplishing communication
5   Burke's characteristic mode of analysis of motivation

Let us first look at Burke's conception of the ground for communication. A colleague of mine has a favorite way of differentiating people on the campus who are concerned in any way with communication. He regularly distinguishes between the Gregory Hall rhetoricians and the Lincoln Hall rhetoricians. Without giving him too much credit, I might take this differentiation as a way into Burke's analysis of the basis for communication. Let us assume that I take Professor Braden[8] as a representative of the Louisiana rhetoricians and I shall use myself as representative of the Illinois rhetoricians. We shall start out by recognizing a generic divisiveness, that is, there are two separate biologic organisms involved. We are animals with requirements for the satisfaction of physical needs, food, shelter, etc. Our animal nature grounds us in property, whether it be a house on

Ursuline Drive or an apartment on Springfield Avenue, a desk in Peabody Hall or a book shelf in Lincoln Hall. Out of our productive capacities will grow certain differences, even as we are both engaged in the co-operative activity of educating students.

Because Professor Braden and I are presumably rational, still other aspects of divisiveness show themselves. Although we have in common as rational animals a symbol using capacity, some differences show themselves. Professor Braden, for instance, knows something about the Chi square; I do not. Professor Braden knows something about Professor Wise's[9] theory of language; I do not. I know something about the history of rhetoric at Illinois; Professor Braden does not. I know something about Kenneth Burke; I am not sure whether Professor Braden does or not. In other words, there is a difference in intellectual or rational property, too.

Hence, we have in a society whose direction is co-operation, people who are apart. Different nervous systems, through language and the ways of production erect various communities of interests and insights, social communities varying in nature and scope. Out of the division and the community arises the universal communicative situation.

The basis of communication, then, lies in generic divisiveness which, being common to all men, is a universal fact about them prior to any divisiveness caused by social classes. Out of this divisiveness emerges the cause for linguistic communication; hence communication is compensatory to division.[10] To understand Burke, one must never let go of the stress he places on two aspects of man: his animal nature, which grounds him in physical property; his rational nature, or symbol using capacity, and the differences that result from that.

Let us consider the nature of communication. "In its essence," Burke says, "communication involves the use of verbal symbols for purposes of appeal." Thus, communication splits formally into three elements: speaker, speech, and spoken-to, with the speaker so shaping his speech as to commune with the spoken-to. This purely technical pattern is the pre-condition of all appeal. And, "stand-offishness" or let us say, separateness, is necessary to the form, because without it appeal could not be maintained. For, if union is complete, what incentive could there be for appeal? There can be courtship only insofar as there is division.[11]

One notices that Burke makes "appeal" the essence of communication. This, in turn, he labels the *rhetorical* function of language. Rhetoric is the mode of appeal essential for bridging the conditions of estrangement natural to society as we know it (be it primitive, feudal, bourgeois, or socialist) with its reliance upon the devices of magic, pantomime, clothes, or pastoral. The use of words by human agents to form attitudes or to induce actions in other human agents is a rhetorical use of words. It is *"rooted in an essential function of language itself,"* namely *"the use of language as a symbolic means of inducing cooperation in beings that by nature respond to symbols."*[12]

It is not uncommon to think of rhetoric as an overlaid prettiness in discourse, or the blandishments of a prose piece. This sort of meaning is implied in the phrase "mere rhetoric," and it is probably the most commonly held opinion of what rhetoric is. Burke tends to think of rhetoric in terms of the development of language. Language, he argues, developed because of the need for co-operative action. Hence, from its beginning it has been marked by the weightings and emotional loadings that characterize human activity in general. In other words, neither in its beginnings nor at any time has language been a neutral instrument. Language is an act upon a scene; it contains the colorings of human purpose, choice, feeling. It is now as it has always been, an adjunct of action, a way of encompassing situations. Thus, Burke suggests that such naming as friend, foe, automobile, or bastard not only name things, but in growing out of experience, suggest appropriate courses of action. Hence, Burke would say wherever there is meaning there is persuasion, and wherever there is persuasion there is rhetoric.[13]

Persons who are familiar with Malinowski's sizing up of primitive cultures,[14] or of I. A. Richard's discussion of the nature of language and meaning,[15] will not find this notion of rhetoric particularly unique. The linguistic way for getting things done is rhetoric. When language operates to induce action or attitude, which is incipient action, it is acting rhetorically. It is an ingredient present in all language since language using is an act. The

scientific use of language is "preparation for action"; the deliberately rhetorical speech is inducement to action or attitude; poetic
use of language is a kind of action in and for itself.[16]

There has been a tendency in the past for people to think of
rhetoric as calculated use of language and linguistic resources.
Burke's concept of rhetoric would eliminate this. He would say
that so long as man uses language symbols at all, he cannot help
being rhetorical; for the vocabularly he uses is a weighted vocabulary, and inducement to attitude or action may take place
where little deliberate design is apparent. For instance, Professor
Gray[17] may say to me, "Come over and join us in the most progressive venture of the age." On the other hand, I may size up
the situation and quite alone long to join the Louisiana rhetoricians, through no deliberate design at all.

We turn now to a third consideration. How much does Burke
bring within the scope of rhetoric? As a preliminary statement,
one might say that Burke would bring within the scope of rhetoric
any and all symbolic resources that function to promote social
cohesion, and all symbolic resources that induce attitude or action. Now this is not to say that a book on mathematics could
just as well be thought of as a book on rhetoric. But it does say
that to the extent that a book on mathematics has meaning, it is
a preparation for action, hence has a rhetorical ingredient in it.
It says that the fire which has the capacity to act on paper and
destroy it may have the capacity to act on me; hence, it too has
a rhetorical ingredient. It says that if a magnolia lures me to it
by its beauty, it is acting on me rhetorically. It also says that
when an Alpinist like Burke lures me by challenge and defeat
to grapple with him to the end of understanding him, he is acting
on me rhetorically. It says that when the anthropologist concerns
himself with the use of magic as a means of promoting social
cohesion in early tribal groups, he has entered the rhetorical field,
or when the social psychologist studies the cohesiveness of a
society, and the means by which this cohesiveness is implemented,
he is examining rhetorical matters. It means that when the poet
or the playwright, or the short story writer, or speaker is manipulating symbols to the end of inducing an attitude in the reader,
or to make the reader say, "How moving," he is making language

perform a rhetorical function. Thus, Burke would say, that one "can place in terms of rhetoric all those statements by anthropologists, ethnologists, individual and social psychologists, and the like, that bear upon the *persuasive* aspects of language, the function of language as *addressed*, as direct or roundabout appeal to real or ideal audiences, without or within."[18]   In other words, I can place in terms of rhetoric the "me" that I cajoled into giving this talk on Burke as well as the "you" whom I am trying to lead to a better understanding of Burke.

Let us move on to the next aspect of Burke's thought, namely, How does appeal take place? In the *Journal of General Education* for April, 1951, under the title, "Rhetoric Old and New," Burke makes this remark: "If I had to sum up in one word the difference between the 'old' rhetoric and a 'new' (a rhetoric reinvigorated by fresh insights which the 'new Sciences' contributed to the subject), I would reduce it to this: The key term for the old rhetoric was 'persuasion' and its stress was upon deliberate design. The key term for the 'new' rhetoric would be *'identification,'* which can include a partially 'unconscious' factor in appeal."[19] Identification at its simplest is a deliberate device, as when the politician seeks to identify himself with his audience by saying, "I was once a farm boy myself." In this respect, its equivalents are plentiful in Aristotle's *Rhetoric*. But identification can also be an end, as when people earnestly yearn to identify themselves with some group or other. Here they are not necessarily being acted upon by a conscious external agent, but may be acting upon themselves to this end. In such identification, there is a partially idealistic motive, somewhat compensatory to real differences or divisions, which the rhetoric of identification would transcend.

Now, to handle this central doctrine of identification, I shall have to introduce a concept that has been troublesome to philosophers for generations. Burke is concerned with the principle on which appeal rests; he is only peripherally interested in the technologies and devices that grow out of the principle. In Burke's language, when one *identifies* himself with someone else, or with something else, he becomes *consubstantial* with it. "A doctrine of *consubstantiality*, either explicit, or implicit, may be necessary to

any way of life," says Burke. "For substance in the old philosophies, was an *act;* and a way of life is an *acting-together;* and in
acting together, men have common sensations, concepts, images,
ideas, attitudes that make them *consubstantial.*"[20]

The word *substance* is not unfamiliar to most of us, but what
it refers to probably is. The language of everyday speech will
yield an unsettling array of uses of it. Doctors speak of a foreign
substance in the blood. The politician and school man will say,
"Now the substance of the doctrine is so and so." And some one
will say, "Professor Wise's theory of language is substantially the
same as Professor Gray's."

If you look at Aristotle, you will find among other things that
a stone is a substance. If you look in Spinoza, you will find only
God is a substance. In the main, perhaps, the ancients used this
term to denote the indestructible, enduring identity in things,
that which is the same in their changing forms and in the differences of their manifestations. As has been amusingly remarked,
the word refers to the "thingness" of a thing.

In the first place, then, *substance* involves the idea of identity,
separateness, uniqueness. One might ask the question: What is
a society? A person who accepts the doctrine of substance would
not be satisfied if someone answered: It is an aggregate of people. He would insist that there is a unity of idea or principle
which gives coherence to the parts. Someone might ask: What is
a cell? and receive the answer: Well, it's a mass of protoplasm.
But a substance thinker would say, No, the substance of a cell is
not protoplasmic stuff but the law according to which the cell
divides, reforms, and divides again.

Curiously enough, as Locke and others before him have
pointed out, etymologically, the word *substance* means to stand
under; hence, it involves a paradox of thinking of a thing both
in terms of what a thing is in itself, and what a thing is extrin-
sically. For instance, a child both is and is not one with its
parents. It is both part of and separate from its parents. Even
while it is consubstantial with its parents it is at the same time
a distinct substance in its own right, surrounding itself with
properties of its own, like hot rods and hoola hoops.[21]

How does the principle of consubstantiality work out rhetorically? Suppose, I decide to praise God, a distinct substance.

God, at the same time, may have got himself identified with one system of property or another, like the capitalistic system. Thus, I may identify myself with God as a principle of good, but fail to identify myself with God's external connections. Suppose I praise the Jupiter rocket, a distinct substance, but it is a product of science and science has got itself connected with nuclear warfare. In other words, every distinct substance participates in a wide range of activity. Identification is a word which covers the whole range of activity. A shepherd as shepherd acts for the good of the sheep, in which case one can identify himself with his goodness, but he, in turn, identifies himself with a project that is raising sheep for the black market, in which case identification may fail to take place. The notion of substance has wide range indeed. It may move around between idealistic and materialistic frames of reference. For instance, if men are separate in body, they may be shown to be united in spirit. If one wants to sanction a nation's extension of its physical dominion, the audience may be led to identify itself with the spreading of ideals. If the University of Illinois is in a shambles, one may talk of its common purpose. If there is a struggle over the means for accomplishing something, one may identify the audience with ends.

Those of you who are familiar with Aristotle's injunctions in the *Rhetoric* will remember he remarked that in praising a man you must make the hearer believe that he shares in the praise either personally, or through his family, or profession, or somehow.[22] Such an observation, of course, easily translates itself into terms of the doctrine of substance. Identification may take place in principle, or through the whole range of associated properties and interests. Persuasion involves communication by the signs of consubstantiality or commonality.

Although identification appears to take place from the groundings of language in properties of various sorts, intellectual or material, one must not lose sight of the fact that, according to Burke, language has a property or resource of its own. Although words are aspects of a wide communicative context, much of which is not verbal at all, yet words have their own peculiarity. Now, one may ask: What is this nature of their own that words have? Burke would argue that language at a minimum is a mode of *transcension;* hence it has dialectical resources in itself and of itself for supporting identifications. Whereas communication is grounded in property, it is also grounded in dialectic. To see this dialectical feature one might note the character of such words as Professor Wise, scientist, son of God. What this means is that language has the capacity to keep men apart as separate substances, like Professor Wise, Professor Gray, Professor Braden, etc., but also unite them on the level of idea, men of science, rhetoricians, teachers, and round out the symmetry of union on an even higher level of abstraction, sons of God. I do not mean to endow any of these men with angelic features; I am merely trying to show how language works. This, I presume would account for some of the mystical unions and identifications which are brought about whereby men identify themselves with God, in ultimate union, as for instance, Emerson and Mahatma Ghandi might have been expected to do.

Burke does not throw out the old rhetorical devices that many of us have sometimes thought to be the whole of rhetoric. What he does is to provide a rationale. All of *structure* as we know it, whether in speech, or story, is treated as a mode of identification. It is an appeal to the needs of the audience. One identifies himself by thinking of structure in terms of the psychology of the audience. What one does first in a speech is what the audience might be expected to need first. It is a response to a condition of expectation in the audience; to the extent that structural elements meet this expectation, speaker and audience are one on structural levels.

Style, likewise, is a mode of identification. In its essence it is a mode of "ingratiation."[23] It is a signal of consubstantiality to talk the language of the group. It is a mode of *formal* sharing. Take an example like the following stylistic mechanism: who controls salaries, controls the faculty; who controls the faculty, controls the University of Louisiana; who controls the University of Louisiana controls the quality of education in the state. Burke takes a stylistic vehicle like this to indicate the degree of identification that can be brought about. Once a series of this sort is started, one brings about almost a determination on the part of the audience to participate actually in its rounding out, or in the completion of the series. Figurative language in general is redolent with identifying features.

There is one more stage left in this Alpine climbing, namely, Burke's mode for the critical analysis of motivation, or as he would put it, the critical analysis of human activity as it is reflected in the language situation. His critical apparatus for the examination of motivation and for human conduct in general has caused considerable stir among language students and critics. There is something of a trumpet blare in the name that has been applied to his critical apparatus. He calls it his "dramatistic pentad"—and if that is not enough, his other label is "dialectical substance."

Take as a starting point his observation: "We shall look upon language-using as a mode of conduct and shall frame our terms accordingly." He goes on to say: "We could call this position 'dramatistic' because it thus begins with a stress upon 'action.' " So far, so good. Then he remarks that this approach, instead of being *epistemological* and thus centering on perception, knowledge, learning, etc., shall be an *ontological* one, thus centering on the *substantiality* of the act.[24] In other words, he will be concerned with the language act as a substance. One may note, how central a doctrine of substance is to Burke's whole theory of language and communication.

As I have already indicated, substance refers to the individual thing in its indestructible aspects. For instance, an act is separate from a stone and from other things. And, although each individual act may be different, there is a permanent aspect to all acts. According to Burke this aspect may be talked about in terms of:

1 The *name* of the act itself; for instance, The Compromise of 1850.
2 The *agent* or *agents* who perform the act: Clay, Webster, Calhoun.
3 An *agency,* or means by which the act is performed: language, debate.
4 A *scene,* or background out of which an act grows: political unrest.
5 A *purpose;* to adjust differences between the North and the South.

He would argue that whether one is analyzing a presidential directive, a poem, a piece of scientific writing, a speech, the latest university dramatic production, or The Compromise of 1850, he would be concerned with an act, hence a substance, and this would yield to his critical apparatus. He contends that the problem of motivation in communication is a philosophic one, not ultimately to be solved in terms of empirical science.

The use of the word motive or motivation in Burke was particularly troublesome to me until I asked him about it. Probably it would not have been had I followed out all the clues. I could think of drive, inciting incident, reason, and the host of other synonyms that we use in everyday speech. Throughout Burke's works runs the phrase "motive is but a shorthand word for situation."[25] But I suppose I did not tumble to that. I was aware that historians and scientists alike had become skeptical about the whole notion of causality or motive in terms of simple stimulus and response and had begun to talk in terms of co-ordinates. Thus, I had noted that Hitler could not be thought of singly as the cause of the war, but that the situation could be described as follows: Hitler was an active force, but men served as agents; and guns and planes served as instrumentalities; and land, sea, and air supplied the scene for the purpose of the killing of men. Thus, the *interrelationships* existing among all the factors produced the holocaust of war.

Translated in terms of linguistic motivation this means the language act as a whole *construed as a situation.* In Burke's terms language-using is an act. The motive is the situation in general. Thus, words act upon us as the result of an agent who uses them, the scene out of which they grow, the purpose for which they are intended, and the strategies that are employed in manipulating them. Translating still further, a symbolic situation represents a co-ordination or interrelationship of act, agent, agency, purpose, and scene.

This is Burke's way of finding out something about meaning— i.e., he asks how symbol users perform when they are trying to stir up meanings. Hence, his constant questions: What is language doing? What kinds of persons or actors go with what kinds of acts? What kinds of circumstances go with what kinds of acts? What kinds of purposes go with what kinds of acts? What kinds of agencies are used to perform what kinds of acts? He would argue that the proper approach to the genus man is through the study of symbolic action, as such action takes place in the drama of human relations. These relations are reflected in literary and rhetorical works. One finds out about the symbol user by charting equations in literary and rhetorical works.

Those of you who are familiar with I. A. Richards will remember that in the *Meaning of Meaning* Richards observed suggestively if not definitively: "If we recognize . . . that experience has the character of recurrence, that is, comes to us in more or less uniform contexts, we have in this all that is required for the theory of signs and all that the old theory of causes was entitled to maintain."[26] Burke indicates, of course, that he is quite familiar with all the work of Richards, Ogden, Malinowski, etc. Undoubtedly what he believes he has done is to turn up a critical apparatus for the examination of linguistic experiences, which will in the long run enable him to classify the recurrent experiences of men, as these show themselves in literary works. His quest is to find out something abou' the nature of the symbol-using animal without using the co-ordinates established by laboratory science. By a mode of indexing, he will search a text for the co-ordinates of what goes with what and what follows what in the hope of discovering the recurrent strategies of identification. By constantly asking the question: How is language acting to obtain its ends? he believes that one can find out something about the nature of meaning, motive, human relations in general. By what agent, using what agency, in what scene, for what purpose is language acting to encompass a situation? Language-using of any kind is a response to a situation which arises—and is not only a response, but a strategic response, a stylized response. Thus, if one were analyzing The Compromise of 1850, having named the behavior of the period a compromise, Burke would want to know how language acts in a situation of compromise. Does it act compromisingly? If you label a speech a humorous speech, how is language acting when it acts humorously?

These are the main outlines of Burke's thought on rhetoric and critical procedure. Baffling, inconclusive, he seeks to promote the good life through a better understanding of the resources of language. He started out with a concern for language as a vehicle for creative writing; he went on to see language break down in the years of war and depression in the thirties; he resisted the positivist's view of language in the forties; in the fifties he was ready to start to think in terms of division and union in the *Rhetoric*. His present venture is concerned with language and its personal and ethical resources for promoting the good life.

To the question sometimes raised: Genius or mad man? we need not give an answer. Most of us do not ask that a man be sane. We ask that he be perceptive. For himself, I suppose it would be helpful if he were sane. In one's judgment of painting, it makes little difference whether the painter went mad; or in the judgment of music, whether the composer was blind; or in poetry, whether the poet was experiencing a fine frenzy. This I am quite sure is true: Burke throws off considerably more sparks than most other people with whom I am acquainted in his theorizing about rhetoric, communication, and criticism.

A number of years ago, I had the pleasure of living right next door to the critic, John Crowe Ransom. In talking with him about Burke one day, he referred to Burke as a "saint." On pressing him, I discovered that he had no otherworldly notions in mind in using the term. He was simply referring to the conscientiousness of the man in directing his efforts to promoting the good life here on earth. Most of us in our theorizing about rhetoric, I think, do not always keep this ultimate purpose in mind. I am sure that Burke does, and that is one reason for me, at least, that he has proved provocative and stimulating.

I. A. Richards:
Rhetorical
and
Critical Theory[1]

In 1936, I. A. Richards, the British-American teacher and
critic opened his *Philosophy of Rhetoric* with the remark: "These
lectures are an attempt to revive an old subject. I need spend no
time, I think, in describing the present state of Rhetoric. . . . So
low has Rhetoric sunk that we would do better just to dismiss
it to Limbo than to trouble ourselves with it—unless we can find
reason for believing that it can become a study that will minister
successfully to important needs."[2]

I have been much shocked by the statement for, like most
others in our field, I tended to believe that rhetoricians had
straightened out the meaning of rhetoric and that rhetoric was
far from dead. We have tended to think that our subject fulfills
the last requirement of Richards, namely, that rhetoric minister
"successfully to important needs." Having separated ourselves
from English departments long ago, we have, to some extent,
tended to dismiss notions coming from those quarters as irrele-
vant, and probably intended only for the beginning student in
written composition anyway. However one may rationalize, he
cannot easily dismiss Richards. His institutional and disciplinary
affiliation has nothing really to do with the case.

Even if he had never written a book under the caption of *The Philosophy of Rhetoric*, Richards' other works would have considerable relevance to any student of rhetoric. His lifelong concern has been with the working of words in their many functions, and none of his works leaves any doubt that he is aware of a rhetorical function. As suggested in an earlier lecture, "I do not believe rhetoricians can much longer maintain the position of resting complacently on the Aristotelian conception of rhetoric."

One may trust that knowledge may come through cultivating a capacity for sympathetic and imaginative understanding and not by arrogant rejection of our predecessors. The occasional graduate student who thinks all his predecessors—most of whom he has not read—limited and foolish needs little encouragement. As the fine and wise Judge Learned Hand has noted: "Those ages which ruthlessly break the moulds their forbears laboriously made do not always find freedom in their indeterminism, or reality because their expression is untrammeled."[3] Most of us have little chance of equaling our major predecessors. Nevertheless, our predecessors have not spoken for all time, nor do I believe that they ever intended to speak for all time. They corrected each other with good heart and suggested a pattern of behavior that one may well emulate. Our really valuable predecessors have been men who adjusted to the needs and learning of their time, and all of us recognize that times change.

One of the least useful things about Richards is an aspect of his temperament. In truth, it is somewhat of a triumph of generosity to turn some of his pages. As has sometimes been remarked, the importance of Richards' work on communication has been obscured for many persons by their annoyance at a too-frequent outcropping of the "amateur spirit." A romantic inflation about the significance of the topic, dark hints about the extent of our ignorance, the cataclysm that awaits us unless we accept his new theories, the ready dismissal of all who have gone before him—all these intrude upon the reader to cast suspicion upon the performance. "No matter what a man's standing, and no matter how impressive the substance of his views, you can still regard him from an unassailable vantage-ground if only you happen to observe that he isn't capable of understanding what is said to him."[4] We may at times think that television insults our intelligence, but not many programs make direct charges of our stupidity or lack of comprehension. It is one thing to believe oneself to be stupid and quite another to be told on every page that one is so. Someone recently labeled Richards the "dandy" of the contemporary language scholars, and that is not a bad description of one aspect of him.

Nevertheless, that I. A. Richards is a thoughtful man no one can doubt. Richards has been a profound student of communication and rhetoric. There may be some who can account for the impetus given to the experimental approach to communication in modern times without Richards, but this would be difficult. Much of contemporary experimentalism in rhetoric and communication may be seen as a direct consequence of the impetus given by C. K. Ogden and Richards in 1923, on the publication of their volume, *The Meaning of Meaning*. And chief contemporary experimentalists like Charles Morris at the University of Florida acknowledge the fact.[5] Actually, prior to 1923 psychologists, if they dealt with language at all, considered it a very minor matter. Probably there is no more universally recognized symbol among the experimentalists than the Richards' triangle showing the relationship of the word, the thought, and the object that appeared in *The Meaning of Meaning*.[6] In a sense, the whole contemporary movement in semantics has felt the impact of that symbol. From an unfinished base of a triangle showing that there is no necessary connection between the object and the word, it became an easy matter to phrase the slogan, "The word is not the thing; the map is not the territory." This has been the banner under which the general semanticists have marched for thirty years, at least the modern ones, and its origin is not hard to discover.

But I am not chiefly concerned with the semantic movement, nor even chiefly with the experimentalism of the modern rhetorician. My purpose is simply to examine Richards' attempt to "revive an old subject," in order to discover what may be useful.

One wonders sometimes how a literary man like Richards became immersed in rhetoric. He hints rather darkly that he was shocked into concern. It well may be that he started to wonder what students were getting out of his lectures, as many of us wonder, and found a more subtle way of finding out than most

of us do who wait until examination day. His early experiments
looked innocent enough; they were not even compulsory. He
simply distributed some copies of materials and asked students to
read them and, if they wanted to, after several readings, to comment on what they got out of them. Needless to say, even at
Cambridge, some of those students got out of those materials
some things Richards did not suspect being there. And when
"Woodbine Willie" turned out to be better than John Donne,
Richards was probably so bewildered he concluded he had a
choice between suicide and becoming a martyr to a cause; he
chose the latter. At any rate, he gave up, for a more mundane
and realistic concern, such questions as, What is a poet? Even
Cambridge was not up to metaphysical considerations like, What
is a poet? if it could not even read a poem and find out what it
said. I remember Professor Henry Lee Ewbank of the University
of Wisconsin once telling me that he had asked a student what
the line in Keats's "Ode on a Grecian Urn," "O, attic shape! Fair
attitude!" meant, whereupon the student launched into one of his
best pantomines of the attic back home. I tried out a passage
from Hartzell Spence's *One Foot in Heaven* with similar results.

At any rate, Richards turned to the audience, and in a sense
has been audience-oriented ever since. Actually, Richards' first
work indicated a concern with the audience, for he found the
beauty of poetry to be a state in the audience and not in the
poem in his first work in 1922 on *The Foundations of Aesthetics.*

Not long ago, I talked with a director of the English Home
Program of the British Broadcasting Company who was at Cambridge at the time Richards was conducting some of his early
experiments. He reported that so interested were students in
somebody who was seriously paying attention to what they
thought and felt that two and three hundred people poured into
his classes to listen to him lecture on language and criticism, and,
of course, many of them participated in his experiments.

Richards approaches rhetoric by attacking the concept which
he wishes to restore. "Among the general themes of the old
Rhetoric," he says, "there is one which is especially pertinent to
our inquiry. . . . The old Rhetoric was an offspring of dispute;
it developed as the rationale of pleadings and persuadings; it was
the theory of the battle of words and has always been itself dom-

inated by the combative impulse. Perhaps what it has most to teach us is the narrowing and blinding influence of that preoccupation, that debaters' interest."[7]

Thus does Richards in Olympian fashion seem to dispose of the theory underlying the practice of a Pericles, a Cicero, a Burke, a Churchill, a Roosevelt. Nor does he stop there. "I know no sadder or more disheartening reading than some of the educational theory which leans heavily on psychology," he remarks, "unless perhaps the dreary pages of those masters of Rhetoric who thought themselves perfectly acquainted with the subject when they had learnt only to name some of its tools."[8] Thus, seemingly is dismissed any theory of rhetoric from Aristotle to Whately which had concern with "observing in any given case the available means of persuasion,"[9] or "influencing the *Will*."[10] "What sorts of persuasions are there? and to what ends may we reasonably employ them?" he asks in derision. "This is a question we all hope to dodge."[11] "Persuasion is only one among the aims of discourse. It poaches on the others—especially on that of *exposition*, which is concerned to state a view, not to persuade people to agree or to do anything more than examine it."[12]

Richards roundly condemns most of the theory and the practices of the past. "From *Gorgias* onwards too much in the literature of rhetoric has been sales-talk selling sales-talk; and for very good reasons we are more interested today in defensives against than in aids to eloquent persuasion."[13]

Although the art of conscious controlled interrogation is still man's "best hope," it becomes, according to Richards, a man's "worst bane" when it turns, as it so often does, into a "technique of purblind disputation."[14] Taking part in discussions is "rarely profitable." In view of the immense traditional vogue of the disputation, Richards feels impelled to assert his opposition. No verbal institution, he remarks, "has done more than disputation to frustrate man, to prevent the referential and emotive functions [of language] coming to terms, and to warp the conduct of language—in its highest self-administrating activities most of all." Against the practice of the "puppy war" with words which has been the rule ever since Plato's time, Richards would take his stand. The disputant's interpretations are controlled by immediate specific purposes, he observes. Furthermore, the disputant is usually too busy making his points to see what they are. He is in the worst possible condition to observe what is taking place. "And seeing what is taking place is no small part of the business of learning how to keep things in their places."[15] A controversy, says Richards, is "normally an exploitation of a systematic set of misunderstandings for war-like purposes."[16]

After such a tirade of glittering generalities, one can visualize all the college debaters in America springing to the defense of debate, possibly with just the kind of heat and maneuver that Richards condemns. He must have sized up the Cambridge Union and come away lacking some of the enthusiasm of the "Union man." At any rate, he appeared to be heartily sick of persuasion as heat and commotion, discourse directed by some specific purpose. And I doubt if he would have found many good purposes to which it was directed. We have had healthy tirades against debate and disputation for a long period of time, and the clearing of air that sometimes results has a salutary effect, no doubt. When Richard Murphy, one of my colleagues, in a recent article challenged the ethics of debating both sides of the question, he was deluged with irate responses.[17] There are times when he hopes the air is a bit purer as a result. Disputation is a hardy perennial, and I. A. Richards liked nothing better than to examine hardy perennials. Doubtless there is nothing like an attack on the big problem when one wants a victory; minor skirmishes do not bring the same kind of satisfaction.

From the rhetoric of debate practice, Richards turned to the old rhetorical theory and delivered a blow. The old rhetoric which, according to Richards, began with Aristotle, may perhaps be said to end with Archbishop Whately. Not chiefly Aristotle, but Whately became representative of the old mode of dealing with rhetorical matters, and thus became Richards' chief target. Whately made a good target for he, in his book entitled, *Elements of Rhetoric,* in 1828, had defined his area somewhat narrowly as that of "argumentative composition, *generally,* and *exclusively.*"[18] Whately who, according to Richards, begins by urging that "rhetoric must go deep" ends with merely a "collection of prudential Rules about the best sorts of things to say in various argumentative situations, the order in which to bring out your propositions and proofs and examples, at what point it will be most effective to disparage your opponent, how to recommend oneself to the audience, and like matters." As to all of this, Richards concludes, "no one ever learned about them from a treatise who did not know about them already; at the best, the treatise may be an occasion for realizing there is skill to be developed in discourse, but it does not and cannot teach the skill."[19] This does not sound very much different from some scorching charges made in reference to speech majors in Arthur Bestor's *Educational Wastelands,* an examination of the educational system in this country.[20] Most of you, I am sure, are familiar with the charges. They are perennial, too. So far as Richards was concerned, rhetorical theory in the old books was nothing more than a somewhat chaotic collection of observations made on the ways of lively, venturesome speech and writing. Sections in the old rhetorics which dealt with audiences or with "Hearers in General" "should favour mercy."

Sizing up the attack Richards made on the old rhetoric and noticing his direction in explaining a new rhetoric, H. M. Mc-Luhan suggests that Richards is a "true nominalist son of . . . Agricola, and Ramus."[21] Since the recent publication of the excellent book *Ramus, Method, and the Decay of Dialogue*[22] by Father Walter J. Ong, we have all had an opportunity to refresh ourselves on the position of Agricola and Peter Ramus. Many persons will remember that Peter Ramus separated logic from rhetoric by putting the invention and arrangement canons of the old classical rhetoric into logic, leaving only style and delivery to the province of rhetoric. I doubt really if that description fits what Richards has done, for Richards turns to George Campbell to suggest the foundations of the new rhetoric, and Campbell can scarcely be thought to be a follower of Agricola or Ramus. Campbell retained the old classical line, modified by an application of eighteenth-century psychology, and adjusted the ends of discourse to the psychology of the audience, those ends being to enlighten the understanding, to please the imagination, to move the passions, or to influence the will. Campbell called eloquence "the grand art of communication not of ideas only, but of sentiments, passions, dispositions, and purposes."[23]

"Rhetoric I take to be 'the art by which discourse is adapted to its end,'"[24] says Richards, echoing exactly the well-known definition of Campbell.[25] "What should be among its topics may be seen from the content" of Campbell's book, he says, "a book which deserves more attention than it is likely ever again to receive." Of course, Campbell, like everybody else that Richards surveys, "doesn't fulfill" his program, but had he done so, according to Richards, he would have given us "all we need to know. . .".[26]

The new rhetoric which arises is a rhetoric concerned, not with persuasion merely as a specific end, but with the meanings of statements in any type of discourse. Richards wants the new rhetoric to minister to understanding and to prevent misunderstanding. And it should concern itself with "how much and in how many ways . . . good communication [may] differ from bad."[27] He has argued that the function of rhetoric is to "give insight into the different modes of speech and their exchanges and disguises." Its chief concern is with such things as "statement, full and explicit, or condensed (by abstraction, ambiguity or implication, the hint, the aposiopesis); statement literal or direct, and indirect (by metaphor, simile, comparison, parallel, etc.); suasion, open (from appeal to cajolery) or concealed (either as mere statement or as mere ornament) and so on."[28] Rhetoric should be concerned with "the fundamental laws of the use of language, not just a set of dodges. . . ."[29]

Back in 1923, when *The Meaning of Meaning* appeared, Richards turned to psychology for a proper analysis and understanding of the uses of language and of its maneuvers. At that time he identified two separate uses of language, which he called the logical or referential use of language and the emotive use of language. The failure to detect these wholly different uses, he claimed, led to the confusion in understanding that he saw all around him. He believed that people who talk about the truth of certain statements did not really know what they were talking about, for they do not understand the different dimensions of meaning that language may convey. It is quite possible that he had the clue from another good Cambridge man, Bertrand Russell, who at the beginning of the century, as mathematician and logician, had looked sharply at sentence form and function.[30]

One may illustrate the functions of language that Richards classified by the following sentences:

1   The Mississippi River is 3,960 feet wide at Baton Rouge where the ferry crosses.
2   The lovely Mississippi glides smoothly into the Gulf.
3   Old Man River, that old man river, he just keeps rolling along.

Only one of these sentences is a logical or referential statement according to Richards, for only one can sensibly be tested by reference to objective reality. One can refer to a Mississippi River in objective reality. One can measure its depth and its width with a yardstick. The statement can be determined to be true or false. The second sentence—although there is a specific river which can be referred to and a specific gulf—one cannot refer to "lovely" anywhere in the environment. This is an attitude in someone's head. The sentence is a mixed sentence, with partly referential words in it and partly emotive, and does not yield in all respects to the test of truth or falsehood. It is a rhetorical statement.

The third sentence has no objective truth whatsoever. It is not intended to have any. It is merely a faithful representative of someone's experience and attitude or feeling. These three sentences would give Richards a range from logical or referential sentences through mixed sentences to purely emotive sentences, the latter of which he calls "pseudo-statements."[31] In human discourse one almost never finds the first type of statement outside the sciences. The other two, the mixed and emotive, are the common ones; the one is the type found in almost all discussions pertaining to human problems; the other is commonly used by the poets, and is purely emotive. "There are subjects," says Richards,

mathematics, physics and the descriptive sciences supply some of them—which can be discussed in terms of verifiable facts and precise hypotheses. There are other subjects—the concrete affairs of commerce, law, organization, and police work—which can be handled by rules of thumb and generally accepted conventions. But in between is the vast *corpus* of problems, assumptions, adumbrations, fictions, prejudices, tenets, the sphere of random beliefs and hopeful guesses; the whole world, in brief, of abstract opinion and disputation about matters of feeling. To this world belongs everything about which civilized man cares most. I need only instance

> ethics, metaphysics, morals, religion, aesthetics, and the discussion
> surrounding liberty, nationality, justice, love, truth, faith and knowl-
> edge to make this plain. . . . We cannot profitably attack any opinion
> until we have discovered what it expresses as well as what it states,
> and our present technique for investigating opinions must be admit-
> ted, for all these middle subjects, to be woefully inadequate.[32]

The job of the rhetorician, according to Richards, is to detect
differences in statements, types of meaning that reside in them.

Richards' questioning about language uses and maneuvers lies
in an area where rhetoricians have been weakest. Since the nineteenth century, one may notice that almost none of our textbooks
gets very close to an examination of language. B. F. Skinner has
observed that rhetoricians began with a close analysis of language, classifying hundreds of language structures.[33] Even as
late as Whately in the nineteenth century, there was a carry-over
of a rather close examination of language features. Since that
time, our textbooks have been constantly watering down the
handling of language. If one has ever confronted a group of
graduate students with conventional terms for describing language maneuvers, such as metonymy, synechdoche, etc., he will
have noticed how mysterious the terms seem to be. No one
seriously considers the restoration of the ancient system for the
analysis of language; but that we need some sort of substitute
may not be doubted. However limited the Richards system is,
it may be a step in the right direction. Many language scientists
have picked up the clue. Viewing language as a system of signs
as Richards does, Charles Morris, for instance, has attempted to
amplify the Richards classification into four categories—informa-
tive signs, valuative signs, prescriptive signs, and formative
signs.[34] Actually the Morris system of analysis corresponds to
the features which Richards claims to be inherent in any discourse, namely, the symbolizing of reference, the expression of
attitudes toward listeners, the expression of attitudes toward
what one is talking about (or referent), and the promotion of
effects.

There is little doubt that in our concern with speeches, and in
our concern with debating, we have sometimes made rhetoric
appear to be a set of dodges and gadgets. There are still some
around who believe its concern is with making the worse reason

appear the better. Richards' protest against the old rhetoric, as
a concern with persuasion merely, is not much different from the
protest of Donald Lemen Clark, a faithful member of the Speech
Association of America who cannot be thought to be much of a
heretic. In 1950, Clark remarked: "Let us . . . envisage rhetoric
as the training of young people to take their place in a human
society where all transactions are conducted through the medium
of language. I believe that if we adopt a broader definition of
rhetoric and teach rhetoric with our eyes on the humane goals
set up by Isocrates and Cicero, we are likely to persuade our
academic colleagues that Rhetoric is today—as it was in antiquity
—a truly liberal art." It is "rhetoric alone, as the culminating art
of the arts of language," says Clark, "which is equipped to teach
the student how to order his language, to order his thought in
speech and in writing." Clark goes on to say, ". . . we still in-
herit the narrow view of rhetoric which Aristotle condemned as
lacking sufficient enrichment in logic. We have also inherited
the less narrow tradition of Aristotle, but still a narrow tradition
because he limited rhetoric to the art of persuading a popular
audience, turning away from the enrichment of the other arts
and sciences. There is always the danger that rhetoric may suffer
from malnutrition for lack of the minerals and vitamins of literature and logic, of history and philosophy, of the political and
social sciences."[35]

To account for understanding and misunderstanding, to study
the efficiency of language and its conditions, is Richards' role for
the new rhetoric. This, he believes, is to face squarely the fact
that meanings do not reside in words, but in responders to words,
and responders may be responding to several different dimensions
of language. We have to renounce the view says Richards, "that
words just have their meanings and that what a discourse does is
to be explained as a composition of these meanings—as a wall can
be represented as a composition of its bricks. We have to shift
the focus of our analysis and attempt a deeper and more minute
grasp and try to take account of the structures of the smallest
discussable units of meaning and the ways in which these vary
as they are put with other units."[36]

By 1923, Richards had concluded that the culture of stable
meanings was gone. This was long before our State Department

would have had a chance to agree. Scores of our State Department men know that a single word, present or absent, in a Russian communiqué alters the literal sense of what is being said. The meaning discovered by the State Department is not the same kind of meaning as that discovered by the party member. Most of us remember that Nazi social democracy rang no bells with us, but that it rang bells in Hitlerian youth cannot be doubted. If one cannot understand what is being said, or if what is being said is capable of scores of interpretations, then minute examination of language becomes imperative. Would the ancients, with all their wisdom, have been ready to understand the guilt-by-association tactic used in our time, and contained in such a phrase as, "Alger, I mean Adlai"? I can well imagine a critic of even fifty years ago, on encountering the tactic in a speech, believing he had discovered a stenographic error, or perhaps, an innocent slip of the tongue. He may have been wise enough to think he had a figurative expression, an instance of epanalepsis, or something of the sort, but that he would have thought of the smear usage is not likely. Two supporting words in juxtaposition suggest a whole ideology, with all the rhetorical force that might be weighted against a man associated with that ideology.

"It is plain," says Richards, "that most human utterances and nearly all articulate speech can be profitably regarded from four points of view," or dimensions. "Four aspects can easily be distinguished." These he calls, Sense, Feeling, Tone, and Intention. "We speak *to say something*," he remarks, "and when we listen we expect something to be said. We use words to direct our hearers' attention upon some state of affairs, to present to them some items for consideration and to excite in them some thoughts about these items." This is what Richards means by Sense, and, as may be readily recognized, it pertains to referential use of language. "But we also, as a rule, have some feelings *about these items*, about the state of affairs we are referring to. We have an attitude towards it, some special direction, bias, or accentuation of interest towards it, some personal flavour or coloring of feeling; and we use language to *express* these feelings, this nuance of interest. Equally, when we listen we pick it up, rightly or wrongly. . . ." Thus, another dimension of meaning, is *Feeling*, or attitude toward our references. "Furthermore, the speaker has ordinarily *an attitude to his listener.* He chooses or arranges his words differently as his audience varies, in automatic or deliberate *recognition of his relation to them.*" This is the *Tone* dimension of meaning, in terms of which Richards believes many of the secrets of style could be shown to reside. "Finally . . . there is the speaker's intention, his aim, *conscious or unconscious,* the effect he is endeavouring to promote." Ordinarily, says Richards, a person "speaks for a purpose, and his purpose modifies his speech." An understanding of this dimension of purpose or intention is "part of the whole business of apprehending . . . meaning." According to Richards, unless we know what a person is trying to do, we can hardly estimate the measure of his success. Sometimes, Richards notes, a speaker will intend no more than to state his thoughts, or to express his feelings about what he is thinking, e.g., Hurrah, Damn, or to express his attitude to his listener. Frequently his intention operates through and satisfies itself in a combination of the other functions. Yet it has effects not reducible to their effects. It may govern the stress laid upon points in an argument, for example, shape the arrangement, and even call attention to itself in such phrases as "for contrast's sake," or "lest it be supposed." Nevertheless, it "controls the 'plot' in the largest sense of the word," and is at work whenever the author or speaker is hiding his hand.

"The all-important fact for the study of literature—or any other mode of communication—is that there are several kinds of meaning. . . . Whether we are active, as in speech or writing, or passive, as readers or listeners, the Total Meaning we are engaged with is, almost always, a blend, a combination of several contributory meanings of different types."[37]

In our critical practice, I believe it is true that in our effort to show the influence of rhetoric on history, or to show that the speaker accomplished his purpose, we do not scrutinize all the resources of meaning as much as we might. In this respect, I believe Richards has done yeoman service in reminding us. "The whole apparatus of critical rules and principles," he says, "is a means to the attainment of finer, more precise, more discriminating communication."[38] Although he is aware that he may seem to be exaggerating, he says that this is so. Whether so or not, few of us should doubt that one of our functions as rhetoricians is, or should be, assistance in obtaining more discriminating communication. "In criticism," says Richards, "the difference between better and worse utterances is in design. Poor speech and writing is poor either because it is not attempting anything worth trying or because it is inefficient."[39] Critics often demonstrate "unmistakable confusion between value and communicative efficacy."[40] A complete critical statement would be a statement about the values of experience and also a statement about communicative efficacy through which experience is revealed.

In the June, 1958 issue of *Speech Monographs*, one will find an abstract of a dissertation done by Charles Redding, now of Purdue University. It has a long title: "A Methodological Study of 'Rhetorical Postulates' Applied to A Content Analysis of the 1944 Campaign Speech of Dewey and Roosevelt," and was done at the University of Southern California. I happen to know that this thesis was a long time in the making, not entirely because of the usual procrastination of graduate students, but because Redding was looking for a methodology. After investigating the current methodologies in rhetoric, Redding concluded that "traditional methodologies have especially failed to provide adequate means for studying speech content."[41] He could have gone on and noted what is apparent to most of us, that is, that current methodologies have especially failed also to provide adequate means for studying language in general.

Redding started to do a conventional dissertation, using conventional methods, but ended with a dissertation scientifically oriented. He had discovered as others have discovered that traditionally oriented rhetoricians often lack an orderly—and one might say—demonstrably useful method for the analysis of speeches. We patch together bits from Aristotle, bits from Quintilian, bits from propaganda analysis, bits from modern textbooks in persuasion or logic and then approach rhetorical matters, usually neglecting expository discourse altogether.

One of the most useful things about I. A. Richards for the traditionally oriented rhetorician is his demonstration of the possibility of finding an orderly methodology for the analysis of discourse. I do not mean that Richards' method should be adopted, that we take his method for the analysis of the types

of meaning in discourse, or his method for pointing out meta-
phorical maneuvers in language. What I do mean is that we also
should be looking for an orderly methodology. The experimentalists, by necessity, have moved in the direction of exactness and
system, and for this they are to be congratulated. But by far
the greatest number of dissertations are still being done with
some form of traditional methodology. Year after year our dissertations go through the ritual of discovering logical, emotional,
and ethical proof in speeches. Year after year, language, if it is
handled at all, gets a few words about rhetorical questions, antith-
esis, and metaphors, with very little rationale. In an analysis
of Adlai Stevenson's campaign speeches of 1952, Stevenson
emerged with a "middle" style, "neither plain nor grand."[42] Hoary
with age, the classification meets the test of time, but I am not
sure that it reveals much of a search for a methodology adapted
to the needs of our times.

I can think of no more rewarding week's work for a rhetorician
than that which might be used in coming in contact with a mind
like Richards' in such things as *The Meaning of Meaning, Practical Criticism, Interpretation in Teaching,* or *Speculative Instruments.* Richards has attempted to keep abreast of the learning
of the last two thousand years and has applied his knowledge
to an area of activity in which we as rhetoricians are notoriously
weak, the area of methodology—methodology not merely for the
analysis of persuasive discourse, but methodology for the ordering
of all types of discourse.

Chapter VIII

George Bernard Shaw: Rhetorician and Public Speaker

Bernard Mandeville in the eighteenth century wrote in "The Fable of the Bees":

> . . . there is no Part of Learning but some Body or other will look into it, and labour at it, from no better Principles, than some Men are Foxhunters, and others take delight in Angling. Look upon the mighty Labours of Antiquaries, Botanists, and the Vertuoso's [*sic*] in Butterflies, Cockleshells, and other odd productions of Nature; and mind the magnificent Terms they all make use of in their respective Provinces, and the pompous Names they often give, to what others, who have no Taste that way, would not think worth any Mortal's Notice. Curiosity is often as bewitching to the Rich, as Lucre is to the Poor; and what Interest does in some, Vanity does in others; and great Wonders are often produced from a happy Mixture of both.[1]

Somewhere in Mandeville's explanation of the motivation behind scholarship there must be a reason for my interest in Bernard Shaw as rhetorician and public speaker. In any event, whatever the obscure reasons may be, I like Shaw, perhaps because I share his faith in public discussion and debate. During the last presidential election candidates appeared on a common platform to explain their ideas and expose their beliefs. Shaw would have hailed the scheme with one of his multitudinous letters to the press. No stauncher advocate of public discussion has ever existed. Only recently one of the members of the speech department of Louisiana State University moderated a debate between students of the University of Havana and students of Georgetown University. Shaw would have gone on record as saying there is no other way for young men to get a liberal education at all except by the threshing machine of controversy over matters of vital concern. Some time ago the philosopher Houston Smith of the Massachusetts Institute of Technology argued that knowledge alone does not generate commitment and that liberal arts colleges must make provision for those experiences in controversy in which commitments are bred. To that Shaw would have said in his most pontifical fashion: You must not claim originality for that idea; I, Bernard Shaw, a man with 20–20 vision, a man with the most superior mind in Britain put that into your head a hundred years ago. And who knows, maybe he did. At any rate, a look at this social "engineer" of the nineteenth and twentieth centuries from the point of view of his methods may not be amiss.

When Bernard Shaw spoke through the pages of the *Quarterly Journal of Speech* in December, 1949, he made it clear that the Shavian essayists are not really to be read or listened to for his sake, but for their own sake. So persons can assume that I am to be listened to for my sake and that Shaw is "perfectly innocent" of anything I might have to say about him.[2] In fact, I am not saying anything about the real Shaw at all, for he has told us, he was "not a real person; he is a legend created by myself; a pose, a reputation."[3] The real Shaw was not a bit like anything anyone can discover about him.

On October 11, 1931, Shaw made his first radio address exclusively to an American audience, or, at least, someone identifying himself as Bernard Shaw said: "Hello, America!—Hello, all my friends in America! How are all you dear old boobs who have been telling one another for months that I have gone dotty about Russia?"[4] Cicero would undoubtedly have given him a D for his disregard of the dictum that one should conciliate his audience. And on the basis of such flippancy, doubtless Quintilian would not have risked including him in the category of "good men."

In many respects, Shaw's salutation reflects the confident icono-
clasm, the rhetorical heresy of the mode of rhetoric and public
speaking that characterized him all his life. If somewhat uncon-
ventional, his manner, nevertheless, grew out of a fairly well
formulated theory of rhetoric, and out of a practice that was extensive and successful, particularly if success is measured in
terms of attention.

When Shaw talked to America in 1931, he had fifty-two years
as a public speaker behind him. His interest in speaking went
even beyond those fifty-two years of experience; for, as a boy of
eighteen and a half, still in Ireland, he first emerged in writing
as a rhetorical critic. Dwight L. Moody and Ira Sankey, the
American evangelists were conducting a revival in Dublin in
1875, and Shaw joined the throngs at the Exhibition Building to
hear them, sending out his first letter to the press immediately
afterward.

Mr. Moody's oration was "characterized by an excess of vehement assertion and a total absence of logic," he said. Such
"awakenings" should be addressed to "the outcasts of the street"
and not to those "members of the aristocracy who by their presence . . . are merely diverting the evangelistic vein into channels
where it is wasted. . . ." Respecting the effect of the revivals on
individuals, Shaw wanted to assert that they have a "tendency
to make them highly objectionable members of society. . . ."[5]
Little could he have known that at a later date his "awakenings,"
too, would sometimes be looked upon as exhibitions of delinquency threatening to a stable society.

Shaw's speaking career began in 1879, at the age of twenty-
three, four years after he had arrived in London. After five false
starts at novel writing, he joined a debating society. The society
was called the Zetetical Society and was a junior copy of the old
Dialectical Society, which he later joined. Both societies were
concerned with discussion of John Stuart Mill's "Essay on Liberty." Members of the Zetetical Society listened to speakers and
then threw the floor open for crossfire inquisition and debate.
The tone of the debates was strongly individualistic, atheistic,
Malthusian, evolutionary, Ingersollian, Darwinian, Herbert Spen-
cerian. Huxley, Tyndall and George Eliot were on the shelves
of all the members. Socialism was regarded as an exploded fal-

lacy, and nobody dreamt that within five years it would revive, snatch away this younger generation, and make this self-consciously advanced group of thinkers re-think their premises.[6]

In the Zetetical Society Shaw began his first assault on an audience in a "condition of heartbreaking nervousness."[7] Joining the Zetetical Society was merely the beginning of his habits of joining any society that had its doors open when he wandered the streets of London, waiting for his day to come.

On September 5, 1882, Shaw heard the American single-taxer, Henry George, in a spellbinding oratorical feat at Memorial Hall, London, and was struck "dumb," as he put it. George's speech that night "kindled the fire" in his soul. "It flashed on me then for the first time," he wrote, "that 'the conflict between Religion and Science' . . . overthrow of the Bible, the higher education of women, Mill on Liberty, and all the rest of the storm that raged round Darwin, Tyndall, Huxley, Spencer and the rest, on which I had brought myself up intellectually, was a mere middle-class business. Suppose it could have produced a nation of Matthew Arnolds and George Eliots:—you may well shudder. The importance of the economic basis dawned on me."[8] Thereafter, he attended sessions of the Land Reform Union.

May 16, 1884, he joined a society that had been founded in January of that year for " 'reconstructing society,' based on the competetive system, 'in such manner as to secure the general welfare and happiness.' "[9] Previously he had been attending sessions of the chief socialist group operative at the time, Henry M. Hyndman's Democratic Federation, but did not join it. The reform society he joined in 1884 turned out to be the famous Fabian Society. Before the year ended he was elected to its executive committee and continued as a guiding spirit of the society, along with such social thinkers as Sidney and Beatrice Webb, Graham Wallas, and Sydney Oliver, until 1911. The London branch of the Fabian Society is still going strong, and when I observed its sessions during the winter and spring of 1958, it looked as if it would go on another seventy-five years. Within a year of its founding it became socialistic and has remained so.

Shaw both cut and sharpened his teeth in the Zetetical and Fabian societies, first in the parlors of the members of the societies, then on street corners, in the parks, at the docks, or down on the Thames embankment. But he joined other societies, too—any society that promised intellectual stimulation or afforded him an opportunity to express himself.

Frederick James Furnivall, organizer of societies during the times, put Shaw's name on the list of people interested in founding a Browning Society in 1883, and Shaw abided by an accomplished fact, becoming a faithful attendant of the meetings and an active participant. On October 12, 1883, he showed up to become a member of the Shakespeare Society. On April 14, 1886, he attended the meeting of the newly organized Shelley Society, shocking the members by announcing that he was "a socialist, an atheist, and a vegetarian," just as Shelley had been.[10] He joined a Hampstead Historic Society, a society organized for the understanding of Karl Marx's *Das Kapital,* which met every fortnight between 1884–1889. In this society members alternated at being teacher and taught themselves economics. He participated in alternate weeks in an economic group which later became the Royal Economic Society.[11]

Our "favorite sport," said Shaw, after he had got some skill in debate, "was inviting politicians and economists to lecture to us, and then falling on them with all our erudition and debating skill, and making them wish they had never been born."[12] As a result of his activities in these societies, Shaw developed a kind of undergraduate exuberance and delight in forensic feat, and he never lost the pleasure of intellectually downing an opponent in debate. In these societies he developed the habit of investigating topics, of collecting masses of facts to support any argument, of playing with ideas, of intellectual sparring. In these societies he became the confrere of Sidney Webb, without whom, Shaw says, he would have become merely a literary hack and twaddler. Webb, according to Shaw, had the greatest mind in England and the greatest knowledge of practical economics, and could bring Shaw's fanciful economics crashing to the earth with a hard fact.

Shaw never gave up group activity throughout his life. In 1897, he became a Vestryman and Borough Councilor for the St. Pancras District of London, serving on the Housing, Lighting, Health, Parliamentary, and Drainage committees. Contemplate for a moment this budding playwright sitting at the City Hall discussing drain pipes and sewage disposal, or of a morning sitting in a cold room addressing envelopes to the electorate and in the afternoon composing *Man and Superman*, for that is actually what he did. Shaw later became a member of the governing board of the Royal Academy of Dramatic Art, regularly attending its sessions until he was eighty-five years old. When radio came along, he became chairman for the committee on Pronounciation of English for Announcers. And, of course, he continued work with the Fabian Summer Sessions all his life. In effect, he was a committee man and a parliamentarian in the strictest and most rigorous sense his entire lifetime. He learned how to put a motion, argue its defense, and carry a motion with consummate skill.

In the early days when trying to teach himself the art of public speaking, Shaw chose an interesting method for gaining attention and for getting the floor. In addition merely to joining societies for practice, he hoped to create for himself a public image, for after all he was a newcomer to London. No London version of Madison Avenue advertising agencies was around to assist him, nor probably could they have done much for the tattered and fraying-sleeved young Shaw, with his long, loose form, his nonchalant, quizzical, extemporaneous appearance, his red hair and scraggly beard, his pallid face, and crooked brows. Shaw had very little to recommend him in those early days, except ambition and undiscovered talent. In meetings of the little hole-in-corner societies, instead of casually getting up to ask questions, he sent a card up to the chairman saying, "Mr. Bernard Shaw would like to ask a question."[13] Thus, it appeared that he was at least a man from Mayfair rather than a shy intellectual hoodlum who spent his days in the reading room of the British Museum. This was a way of setting tongues buzzing to find out who the Mr. Bernard Shaw was who ripped an opponent apart. The method worked; for before long, he was known in all the egghead clubs throughout London, mostly as an irrepressible troublemaker, a sharpshooter debater, and a man of colossal egotism, coupled with saucy wit.

He described himself during these years as an "odious argumentative young man who made himself thoroughly unpleasant by contradicting everybody."[14] Beatrice Webb would have agreed with him, calling him "brilliant but disgusting."[15]

By 1898, ensconced in a literary post, he was able to announce with considerable honesty, "I have been dinning into the public head that I am an extraordinarily witty, brilliant, and clever man. . . . [M]y reputation shall not suffer: it is built . . . on an impregnable basis of dogmatic reiteration."[16]

To one of his biographers, Henry Charles Duffin, Shaw once wrote, ". . . you think of me only as a playwright. Yet for every play I have written I have made hundreds of speeches. . . ."[17] Shaw's inveterate club activity gives force to the statement of G. K. Chesterton in his critical study of Shaw in 1910. Announcing that he was not dealing with Shaw the politician and political philosopher, Chesterton remarked: ". . . only let it be remembered, once and for all, that I am here dismissing the most important aspect of Shaw. It is as if one dismissed the sculpture of Michelangelo and went on to his sonnets. Perhaps the highest and purest thing in him is simply that he cares more for politics than for anything else; more than for art or for philosophy."[18] His home was in the inkpot and his heart was on the platform. "I want . . . my platform, my audience, my adversary, my mission," Shaw announced with exuberance as he readied himself to herald the collapse of Hilaire Belloc, a debating champion, "to the four thousand corners of hell."[19] It was the cart and the trumpet for him.

Shaw threw himself into political activity with zest, delivering thousands of speeches of all kinds, to all kinds of audiences, on all kinds of subjects. At least three times a fortnight for twelve years, he made public speeches ranging in length from a few minutes to four hours, to audiences ranging from the casual passerby in Hyde Park to thousands in public halls. Many of these speeches were on socialism. On a reduced schedule after 1898, he continued this activity until 1941, when at the age of eighty-five, he retired from the platform, still in demand to deliver speeches on all types of subjects.

Having first caught the ear of the British "on a cart in Hyde Park, to the blaring of brass bands," one of his earliest open-air attempts was made in speaking to three tramps lying on their backs on the grass, one of whom, without getting up, called out, "ear, ear," when Shaw paused for breath.[20] Henry James could merely mutter, "I could not do it, I could not bring myself to do

it,"²¹ on discovering that Shaw could stop on Clapham Common
and collect sixteen shillings in his hat at the end of a lecture for
the socialist cause, or stop on the Thames embankment, set his
back to the river wall and have a crowd listening to him in no
time. "I persevered doggedly," says Shaw. "I haunted all the
meetings in London where debates followed lectures. I spoke
in the streets, in the parks, at demonstrations, anywhere and
everywhere possible. In short, I infested public meetings like an
officer afflicted with cowardice, who takes every opportunity of
going under fire to get over it and learn his business."²² And this
roofless orator did get over his nervousness and learn his business,
ending by talking in the largest halls in London, haranguing the
comfortable and the wealthy in Carnegie Hall, New York, collecting 8,640 pennies at Usher Hall in Edinburgh, and filling two
streets with an overflow audience who could not get into the
lecture hall in London after the 1914–1918 war.

Let us take Shaw for a moment at the beginning of his career.
It is January 30, 1885, and he is just emerging from his drawing
room obscurity by representing the Fabian Society before the
Industrial Remuneration Conference held that year in London
to discuss the question: "Has the increase of products of industry
within the last hundred years tended most to the benefit of cap-
italists and employers or to that of the working classes, whether
artisans, labourers or others? And in what relative proportions
in any given period?" Shaw spoke on the third day of the conference to the question: "Would the more general distribution of
capital or land or the State management of capital or land promote or impair the production of wealth and the welfare of the
community?"²³ When his time came, he mustered his courage
and launched in:

> It is the desire of the President that nothing shall be said that might
> give pain to particular classes. I am about to refer to a modern
> class, burglars, and if there is a burglar present I beg him to believe
> that I cast no reflection upon his profession. I am not unmindful
> of his great skill and enterprise; his risks, so much greater than those
> of the most speculative capitalist, extending as they do to risk of
> liberty and life, or of his abstinence; nor do I overlook his value
> to the community as an employer on a large scale, in view of the

criminal lawyers, policemen, turnkeys, gaolbuilders and sometimes
hangmen that owe their livelihoods to his daring undertakings. . . .
I hope any shareholders and landlords who may be present will accept my assurance that I have no more desire to hurt their feelings
than to give pain to burglars; I merely wish to point out that all
three inflict on the community an injury of precisely the same
nature.[24]

Thus, the ironic, paradoxical, witty Shaw had arrived on a
favorite topic: the thievery of the landlord. From this time on,
Shaw was constantly in demand as a speaker and debater. He
learned to talk without notes on the subjects of Rent, Interest,
Profit, Wages, Toryism, Liberalism, Socialism, Communism, Anarchism, Trade-Unionism, Co-operation, Democracy, The Division of Society into Classes, and the Suitability of Human Nature
to Systems of Just Distribution.[25] Before the Fabian Society, he
delivered theoretical discussions lasting more than two hours
each on "The Economic Basis of Socialism," "Transition to Social
Democracy," and "The Impossibilities of Anarchism." The Fabian
Society also became a sounding board for many of his literary
and ethical pieces. Such a famous essay as the "Quintessence of
Ibsenism," known to all drama critics, was first delivered as a
lecture at the St. James Restaurant July 18, 1890 to a delighted
audience.[26] The preface to his play *Back to Methuselah* was first
sounded out in a lecture on Darwin in 1906, as were prefaces to
many of his plays. "I want to change the ideas of the people of
this country," he said, and he set out to obtain any platform
available.

The socialism that emerges in Shaw's early speeches and lectures is a modified Marxian socialism. It is a brand of socialism
worked out in the Hampstead Historic debating club and in the
Fabian Society. It was adjusted to the British society of the time,
in no sense responsive to wild-eyed revolutionaries. Shaw did not
sanction the Marxian theory of value based on the price of labor,
but stood on the ground marked out by the English economist
Stanley Jevons, that prices are determined by supply and demand. He did not recommend revolutionary tactics to accom-
plish the task of transition to a socialistic society but recommended change within the framework of parliamentary means.

His method was that of permeation of existing liberal institutions
—the Liberal Party, the London Country Council, and the parish
vestries.

Shaw was not an innovator in socialist theory; he was an ex-
positor who could make socialism appeal to common sense in
a manner not only attractive but amusing. Not until 1914, when
he recommended the equal distribution of all income, did he
seem out of line even with his confreres in the Fabian Society.[27]
By this time he had already captivated London by his wit, and
nobody expected him to blow up the Bank of England in order
to execute his plan.

Whether Shaw was attacking the capitalistic system, arguing
for taking the lead off chinaware to keep from poisoning the pro-
letariat, debating G. K. Chesterton, Hilaire Belloc, or R. B. Hal-
dane on religious bigotry, arguing against vivisection, or vaccina-
tion, denouncing the medical profession, the educational system,
or war, preaching a doctrine of creative evolution, or scoffing at
the romanticism of the theater, his method was very much the
same. Eric Bentley has perceptively remarked: "What he says
is always determined by the thought: what can I do to this audience? not by the thought: what is the most objective statement
about this subject?"[28] Conducting a moral, political, philosophic
campaign, as a passionate reformer, Shaw adopted a strategy
that was meant to jolt or shock people into seeing the need for
social reconstruction. "It is always necessary to overstate a case
startlingly to make people sit up and listen to it, and to frighten
them into acting on it. I do this . . . habitually and deliberately,"
he said. His chief function, as he saw it, was to create intellectual
unrest, not to quiet the populace. "Half the curates in the king-
dom," he asserted, "conciliate. . . . Toastmasters conciliate. Public speakers who have nothing to say conciliate. And it is intoler-
able except in the one obvious and complete instance—the street
cry." His object was to bring people to a sense of "sin."[29]

His attitude toward his audience, says his contemporary, Holbrook Jackson, was "that of one who is informing them as much
for their own good as because he is irritated at their remaining
in ignorance of the things they ought to know: a knowledge of
which would in all probability make them more agreeable to him."[30]
This would be an impossible attitude for a public speaker did he

not possess some compensating methods for taking care of the wounded pride of listeners. It is not difficult to imagine what an audience might be inclined to do in the face of such apparent affrontery as the following: "Intellectually I am a snob, and you will admit that I have good ground for that." Or, "With the single exception of Homer, there is no eminent writer, not even Sir Walter Scott, whom I can despise so entirely as I despise Shakespeare when I measure my mind against his."[31] Or, "The reason why I talk so much is not to have to listen to what other people say." Or, "I tower above my equals." Or, Lincoln's democracy in the Gettysburg address is shrouded in "a cloud of humbug,"[32] and Churchill is "hopelessly out of date."[33] Or, "I am always in advance of public opinion." Shaw knew precisely what he was doing—insulting his audience to arouse them. But as we may see later, he had compensating methods.

Contemporaries have remarked that no one ever approached this agile-minded man's ability to produce new arguments for any subject that he discussed, or give new twists to old arguments. Arguing socialism, "You have," he remarked, "no right to say of poverty and illness that they are 'the will of God.'" Say in "solemn Scriptural language that it is a damnable thing, and that you have come to try to put a stop to it because *you* are the will of God."[34] Scientists, instead of delivering a truer truth, he argued, were merely delivering new kinds of lies: "When astronomers tell me . . . that a star is so far off that its light takes a thousand years to reach us, the magnitude of the lie seems to me inartistic."[35] Phonetic spelling was important not because it was easier for children and foreigners but because it would represent a return to the freedom and flexibility of Elizabethan literature. Shakespeare himself believed in phonetic spelling, having spelled his own name six different ways.[36]

The paralyzing impudence of such remarks made even progressive members of an audience feel like conservatives, or at least feel as if they had been caught napping.

Particularly in his Fabian Society days he tended to stake out his ground much like a conventional debater, usually arguing from theoretical grounds until his opponent asked for practical consideration or some show of evidence. He advanced with arguments supported by the hypothetical example, the example

from history, or from general observations and experience. There
is a preponderance of analogy, almost a complete disdain for
figures, a like disdain for authority, other than his own, a welter
of exaggeration, paradox, hyperbole, and bits of dialogue or
scenes to make the speeches come alive. He often concluded
abruptly, like "Goodby, goodby, goodby, always happy to have
an opportunity to annoy you."

Shaw voiced the theory underlying his procedure many times,
but I suspect its most forceful enunciation followed an occasion
in which he dozed off to sleep while listening to a speech of an
American lecturer. On being waked up, Shaw announced with
some conviction: "I defy anyone . . . to remember a single
thing the lecturer said. It was all information. You should never
give information in a lecture; only ideas. Information can be got
in a textbook on the subject." Although Shaw swam in facts and
information, he habitually reserved his facts and information for
the question period—a period which he found one of the most
valuable of any speaking occasion. J. S. Collis has remarked:
"He knows the facts. . . . The factual knowledge accounts for
his unparalleled success during question time at public meetings
—for a display of facts always impresses an audience during
question-time in the same proportion as it bores them during
lecture-time."[37] To strange audiences, his readiness in answering
questions and meeting hostile arguments seemed astonishing
and miraculous.

A chaffing wit was one of his methods throughout life. While
he was a vestryman at the end of the century and early in this
one, he decided to run for the London County Council. Beatrice
Webb enters in her diary for March 7, 1904:

> G.B.S. beaten badly. . . . He certainly showed himself hopelessly
> intractable during the election: refused to adopt any orthodox de-
> vices as to address and polling cards, inventing brilliant ones of his
> own. . . . Insisted that he was an atheist; that though a teetotaler, he
> would force every citizen to imbibe a quartern of rum to cure any
> tendency to intoxication; laughed at the Nonconformist conscience;
> chaffed the Catholics about transubstantiation; abused the Liberals;
> and contemptuously patronized the Conservatives—until nearly
> every section was equally disgruntled. [38]

As he put it, when he felt his command of the sublime would have induced sublimity in the mind of his audience, he at once introduced a joke and knocked the solemn people off their perch.[39] In 1920, he remarked:

> I tell you ladies and gentlemen that the most popular lecture I ever delivered in London was one I delivered at the request of the superior persons at Toynbee Hall who step condescendingly down from the Universities to improve the poor. They told me they had a very poor audience—one of the poorest they could get in White-chapel—and they asked me would I address it: and, when I said yes, they said, "What subject shall we put down?" I said, "Put down this as the subject: 'That the poor are useless, dangerous, and ought to be abolished.'" "I had my poor audience; and they were delighted: they cheered me to the echo. . . ."[40]

In the great City Temple of London, before an audience of church people, he could not, as he said, resist the temptation to tell a profane story. There he depicted a scene in which three Christians were debating the importance of miracles to religion, particularly the miracle of the raising of Lazarus from the dead. The debater who made the greatest impression on him, because he offered the most amusing interpretation, was the one who depicted Christ and Lazarus as having made a deal. Having told his profane story, he deftly turned it into a compliment to the minister who at the time was more concerned with the decline of Christianity than with miracles as the foundation of faith.[41]

Shaw used wit and humor to correct conditions among laborers, to correct social conditions, and to beat down what he thought to be the pomp and circumstance and callousness of the British. He scoffed at the stupidity of the British politician, the British culture set, the British churchmen, British parents, rearing their children to be sheltered misfits, and, of course, thought there was nothing worse than an Irishman, except an American. All Americans were the proprietors of the world, the great, loud, stupid, hand-shaking missionaries who made themselves at home in other people's countries—not only made themselves at home in all the capitals of the world but acted as if they were the official hosts and dignitaries and greeters of visitors to those countries.

"Waggery as a medium is invaluable," said Shaw. "My case is really the case of Rabelais all over again. . . . In order to get a hearing, it was necessary for me to attain the footing of a privileged lunatic, with the license of a jester. . . . My method is to take the utmost trouble to find the right thing to say, and then say it with the utmost levity. And all the time the real joke is that I am in earnest."[42]

"I have been described as a man laughing in the wilderness," said Shaw. "That is correct enough, if you accept me as preparparing the way for better things."[43]

Shaw never took money for lecturing. Accepting no fees, he was free to say anything he wanted, to be as ironic, and as irritating as he wanted to be. Unless you say a thing in an "irritating way, you might just as well not say it at all," he remarked. Attention is given in "direct proportion . . . to indigestibility."[44]

Indigestibility reached amazing heights when he scoffed at the laments over the lives of wealthy Americans going to their death in the sinking of the Lusitania and contrasted the atrocities suffered in Belgium during the First World War. The technique of irritation was turned on Americans in 1931, when he taunted:

> Russia has the laugh on us. . . . We have prided ourselves on our mastery in big business. . . and now we are bankrupt; your President, who became famous by feeding the starving millions of war devastated Europe, cannot feed his own people in time of peace. . . . Naturally, the contempt of the Russians for us is enormous. "You fools," they are saying to us, "why can you not do as we are doing? You cannot employ nor feed your people; well, send them to us, and if they are worth their salt we will employ and feed them." And what can we say in reply but "Who would have thought it?" Pretty feeble that, eh? Too true to be pleasant, isn't it? . . .Some of you were very angry with me for taking a commonsense view of war, which is an affair of glory and patriotism and has nothing to do with commonsense. Well, the British soldiers had no commonsense and went on slaughtering. The French soldiers . . . kept blazing away . . . . The Italian soldiers joined up: and presently the American soldiers rushed in and were the silliest of the lot.[45]

The British refused to print the text of the speech, and did as they had often done, fired back in volleys of criticism. Another of his especially irritating speeches began this way: "Is Britain heading for War? That's what you want to know, isn't it? Well, at present Britain is not heading straight for anywhere. She is a ship without a pilot, driving before the winds of circumstance; and as such she is as likely to drift into war as into anything else, provided somebody else starts the war."[46]

Clearly, a man who used such tactics could not attract the huge audiences Shaw attracted for fifty years were there not traces of graciousness somewhere. He has announced that "public oratory is a fine art" and "like other fine arts, it cannot be practiced effectively without a laboriously acquired technique." Not only the substance of Shaw's arguments reflect laboriously acquired technique, but his mode of presentation also reflects technique.

J. Middleton Murray has observed that Shaw was one of the most adept users of plain or simple style in the English language, although Ezra Pound thought him a "ninth rate artist." When Einstein said that Shaw's words were like Mozart's notes, "everyone of them meant something and was exactly in its proper place," Shaw was flattered for the first time in his life and boasted of the compliment.[47]

Shaw has never been very enlightening to the novice trying to give himself a discipline in style, except to indicate: Go and do as I did by talking to people in the marketplace.[48] With customary braggadocio, he announced, "I never have to think how to say anything in prose. The words come with the thought. I often have to argue a thing carefully to get it right but when I have found the right thing to say it says itself instantly; and matters of feeling don't have to be argued . . . I always tell people that if they can't do three quarters of any art by nature they'd better sweep a crossing."[49] Again he observed: "I have never aimed at style in my life; style is a sort of melody that comes into my sentences by itself. If a writer says what he has to say as accurately and effectively as he can, his style will take care of itself, if he has a style."[50] Again, ". . . a true original style is never achieved for its own sake. . . . Effectiveness of assertion is the Alpha and Omega of style. He who has nothing to assert has no style and can have none: he who has something to assert will go as far in power of style as its momentousness and his conviction will carry him. Disprove his assertion after it is made, yet his style remains."[51] Although Shaw had at his command, the "whole vocabulary of English Literature, from Shakespeare to the latest edition of the Encyclopedia Britannica," and never had to consult a thesaurus "except once or twice" when for some reason he "wanted a third or fourth synonym,"[52] he had a tendency to believe that "pidgin is as useful as the English of Milton, and much more precise. . . . Our craze for standards of correctness," he remarked, "pushed as it is to make any departure from them a punishable moral delinquency, wastes years of our lives."[53]

Shaw disciplined himself in writing by pedantically going about the matter in his first five novels. But not until he took to the platform did he achieve the swift, smooth, pungency that characterizes his later style in both his speeches and his plays.

Observers often attributed his success on the platform to his style. It was a style smitingly direct, with words so ordered as to appear to be going somewhere and would get there quickly. Sentences, although often long, are so jointed, as to provide smooth passage. It is a style capable of rapid utterance and many of his listeners attribute success to his pacing. The avalanche of the perpetual talker is there. It is witty, exuberant, conversational patter, often with the cutting edge of the rapier; it was a fit instrument for oral struggle and combat, for scoring points in debate.

Much as his style contributed to his effectiveness—and this is surely considerably—undoubtedly his voice and delivery made an even greater contribution. When Danny Kaye met Shaw in 1948, he noted that one of the most striking features of Shaw was his "most wonderful voice."[54] Shaw was then at the age of ninety-two. According to him, a music teacher, George John Vandaleur Lee, advised that if he was to do anything at all in public he must create a voice that, even if he spoke rubbish, the people would still be enthralled. And when he spoke rubbish, as he himself remarks, people were sometimes bored by the subject "but fascinated by the speaker." His contemporary, G. K. Chesterton, has remarked: "The first fact that one realizes about Shaw (independent of all one has read and often contradicting it) is his voice. Primarily it is the voice of an Irishman, and then something of the voice of a musician. It possibly explains much of his career; a man may be permitted to say so many impudent things with so pleasant an intonation. But the voice is not only Irish and agreeable, it is also frank and as it were inviting conference . . . no man ever used voice or gesture better for the purpose of expressing certainty; no man can say 'I tell Mr. Jones he is totally wrong' with more air of unforced and even casual conviction."[55] Describing himself, Shaw remarked that "it is to his pedantic articulation that he owes his popularity as a public speaker in the largest halls, as every word is heard with exasperating distinctness."[56]

Voice was almost a passion with Shaw, his secretary Blanche Patch noted.[57] The way the English language was spoken mattered greatly to him. You will recall his tirade in *Pygmalion*, put into the mouth of the note taker at the portico of St. Paul's Church in reference to the voice and utterance of the flower girl, Eliza Doolittle: "A woman who utters such depressing and disgusting sounds has no right to be anywhere—no right to live. Remember that you are a human being with a soul and the divine gift of articulate speech; that your native language is the language of Shakespeare and Milton and The Bible; and don't sit there crooning like a bilious pigeon."[58]

Anyone who ever heard Shaw or listened to his recorded address on "Spoken English and Broken English" is aware that he had a most pleasing voice. When he was a youngster he claims that he had no voice worth talking about. His mother, a singer of some note, gave him lessons in breathing and voice production. Later he came in contact with Chichester Bell, whose father was author of the *Standard Elocutionist*, and who had studied under Helmholtz. Shaw learned the secrets of intonation and became acquainted with the mechanism of the voice and, indeed, with the whole physical basis of sound production in the human organism, and in musical instruments alike. Still later, he studied with Richard Deck, an Alsatian basso profundo, and a pupil of Delsarte. Deck taught him that "to be intelligible in public the speaker must relearn the alphabet with every consonant separately and explosively articulated."[59]

Coupled with the clear, comradely, forceful elocution were gestures that were likewise free and forceful. In some respects, the nature of Shaw's gestural pattern may be suggested by an

anecdote. Some one asked the French sculptor Rodin whether
Shaw spoke French, a language which Shaw claimed to know
a little about. "Ah! no! replied Rodin . . . Monsieur Shaw does
not speak French. But somehow or other, by the very violence
of his manner and gesticulation, he succeeds in imposing his
meaning upon you."[60] Shaw's hands and elbows were often
observed to punctuate his sentences. In other words, his gestures
were free and emphatic.

For a few moments now, let the great "humbug" talk about
himself. On November 28, 1949, I wrote Shaw the following
letter which I shall quote in part: "I seem unable to discover
to what extent a formulated theory of rhetoric dominated your
speaking, particularly in your later years. . . . Did you in your
early years consult any of the well-known manuals on speaking,
as for instance, Bishop Whately's Rhetoric or Logic, or Mill's
Logic? . . . Did you have lessons in elocution other than those
from Richard Deck, the Delsartian? When you attended Wes-
leyan Connexional School, did you study elocution under Chichester Bell's father, author of the Standard Elocutionist?"

I did not expect to hear from him—or if I did—I thought he
might draw blood by a postcard, which was his wont. On December 3, 1949, Shaw's ninety-three year old hand wrote me a
letter in red ink. To my series of questions pertaining to classical treatises in rhetoric, he answered "No"—in fact, he said "No"
five times. He went on to say: "to become an effective public
speaker (assuming that you have something to say) all that is
necessary is to practice the alphabet daily as a singer practices
scales until athletic articulation has become a habit. . . . I learnt
this from an old opera singer who had been taught by Delsarte.
The exercise for each consonant was like this: b, b, b, b, b, Bouy-
ant Billions! crescendo—con explosione, as Meyerbeer put it, or
Verdi fffff. Spit it out hard." It was voice again that he harped
on. Yet, as always, the voice must have something to say.

"I cannot think of anybody whose non-existence would have
made a more profound intellectual difference to this transitional
age of ours," said Laurence Housman, "if a negative can be thus
stated as a positive—than would the non-existence of G. B. S.
Had God, in mistaken mercy, decided not to inflict on us the gibes
and ruthless common sense of this brilliant Irishman, we should

have been—if not a different people (made up of all classes)—a very different 'upper middle class,' and a very different intelligentsia."[61] Housman indicates correctly the class on which Shaw made his greatest impact. It was an age of the single eye-glass, and the little man who wore the single eye-glass had frozen both faith and fun at many tea tables. The Victorians to whom Shaw talked in the early part of his career had their virtues, to be sure, but they also had their inhibitions, their shams, repressions, sentimentalities, insincerities, reticences of speech, and callousness. Shaw ushered in a breezy kind of platform manner, and instead of one neatly polished epigram, carefully timed, such as Oscar Wilde might deliver, the agile-minded Irishman could send them out with spendthrift abandon.

Although Shaw was never dull on the platform, it is a mistake to think that he was invariably successful in accomplishing what he set out to do. "I have produced no permanent impression because nobody ever believed me," said Shaw. And with customary exaggeration, he remarked: "For 48 years, I have been addressing speeches to the Fabian Society and other assemblies in this country. So far as I can make out, those speeches have not produced any effect whatsoever."[62] Remarks of this sort are easy enough to disprove, as Housman's statement and hundreds of similar ones demonstrate. There are such things as the Fabian Society which he helped to keep alive almost as long as he lived. There would be those who think that the Independent Labor Party formed in 1893 is, in part, an outgrowth of the activity of Shaw, the Webbs, and a handful of people who organized the liberal sentiment of England. Then, there is the journal, *The New Statesman*, which he helped to found. One might mention with some facetiousness that the number of people who have learned that there is such a thing as a science of phonetics must run into the millions.

And there may be some indication that the St. Pancras district, where Shaw labored as a vestryman at the end of the century is one of the most erratic of the London city districts. How much of this is due to the lingering spirit of Shaw is a question. On May Day in 1958, the Red Flag was hoisted over the City Hall of St. Pancras, where Shaw once presided. One had a feeling that he would have enjoyed the activity of the next day, when a de-

vout Catholic sprinkled holy water on the stairs in an act of puri-
fication. One had also the feeling as he milled around with the
crowd that Shaw's Mephistophelean spirit still pervaded the area.

During his lifetime the English wavered between wishing he
had never been born and hoping he would never die. In piping
times of peace, particularly, they found him hugely amusing and
exhilarating. People like the philosopher C. E. M. Joad, at Oxford, when he first heard Shaw, reported on Shaw's ability to
bring on fits of priggishness among the student body and to set
them up with so much conceit that they were ready to go and
conquer the world. The draughts that many a student drank at
the Shavian spring were heady enough to put them beside
themselves with excitement.[63] When students at the University
of London asked him to come and deliver one of his characteristic
"impassioned orations," he responded with an oration on "intellectual passion." They gave him a resounding cheer.[64]

Shaw undoubtedly lost some of his power over the middle
classes somewhere in the twenties and in the thirties, when his
speeches seemed to indicate that he himself had lost some faith
in negotiation, compromise, constitutionalism, democracy, and
perhaps, even common sense. His jaunty observation, "Now,
Mussolini, there's a man for you," and his flippant praise of com-
munistic methods of execution to weed out the idle, the lazy, and
the useless seemed more than the English could stomach, however much they were accustomed to his exaggeration, his irony,
his flippancy. During the First World War, the British wanted
to gag him.[65]

Shaw made speeches partly because he knew how to make
them. As one of his fellow-countrymen has said, "The English
imagine that Irish politicians are so hot-headed and poetical that
they have to pour out a torrent of burning words. The truth is
that the Irish are so clear-headed and critical that they still regard rhetoric as a distinct art, as the ancients did. Thus a man
makes a speech as a man plays a violin, not necessarily without
feeling, but chiefly because he knows how to do it."[66]

Shaw did know "how to do it." But coupled with this ability
was the desire of a dedicated man who confidently hoped that
the world might become a better place to live in. His remaining
speeches are the outpourings of an incredibly fully educated

man, a quickwitted master of the language, a comradely Irishman who hoped for better things. Choosing a unique way of making a contribution to the country of his adoption, he has left a contribution to the slim body of wit and humor of the world through his speechmaking as well as through his plays.

In closing I will say what Shaw once said; "You have been kind enough to listen to me. I will take no further advantage."

Notes

Chapter 1

1   Everett Hunt, Review of *American Education: The Thirty-Second Discussion and Debate Manual,* in *The Quarterly Journal of Speech,* XLV (April, 1959), 223.

2   Ralph Barton Perry, "A Definition of the Humanities," in *The Meaning of the Humanities,* ed. Theodore Meyer Greene (Princeton, N.J.: Princeton University Press, 1938), 4.

3   *Ibid.,* 4, 5. Cf. "Of the Education of Children," *The Essays of Michel de Montaigne,* trans. and ed., Jacob Zeitlin (3 vols.; N.Y.: Alfred A. Knopf, 1934), I, 131–32.

4   Zeitlin (trans. and ed.), *The Essays of Michel de Montaigne,* 132.

5   Seneca *Epistles* xxxiii. 2; see, *ibid.,* Notes to Ch. XXVI, p. 335.

6   Zeitlin (trans. and ed.), *The Essays of Michel de Montaigne,* 132.

7   See Erwin Panofsky, "The History of Art as Humanistic Discipline," in Greene (ed.), *The Meaning of the Humanities,* 91.

8   Everett Hunt, "Rhetoric as a Humane Study," *The Quarterly Journal of Speech,* XLI (April, 1955), 114.

9   Cited in Panofsky, "The History of Art as a Humanistic Discipline," 92.

10 *Time,* LXV (Feb. 28, 1955), 42; see also, E. D. Baltzell, "Bell Telephone's Experiment in Education: Institute of Humanistic Studies for Executives," *Harper's,* CCX (March, 1955), 73–77.

11 *Rhetorica,* tr. W. Rhys Roberts, *The Works of Aristotle,* ed. W. D. Ross (11 vols.; Oxford: The Clarendon Press, 1924), XI, 1. 2. 1355b.

12 Allen Tate, *The Forlorn Demon: Didactic and Critical Essays* (Chicago, Ill.: Regnery, 1953), 100.

13 *Ibid.*, 104.

14 *Ibid.*, 104, n.3.

15 James Madison, *The Journal of the Debates in the Convention Which Framed the Constitution of the United States, May–September, 1787,* ed. Gaillard Hunt (N.Y. and London: G. P. Putnam's Sons, 1908), II, 389–91, *passim.* The speech was read for Franklin by James Wilson, delegate from Pennsylvania.

16 *Congressional Globe,* 1st sess., 31st Cong. (Washington, D.C.: John C. Rives), XIX, Appendix part 2, p. 1413.

17 Joel Chandler Harris, *Life of Henry W. Grady Including His Writings and Speeches* (New York: Cassell Publishing Co., 1890), 92.

18 *Ethica Nicomachea,* trans. W. D. Ross, *The Works of Aristotle,* ed. W. D. Ross (11 vols.; London: Oxford University Press, 1915), IX, I. 4. 1095b.

19 Richard Murphy, "The Speech as Literary Genre," *The Quarterly Journal of Speech,* XLIV (April, 1958), 127.

20 *Ibid.*, 127.

21 Bess Sondel, *The Humanity of Words* (Cleveland and New York: The World Publishing Co., 1958), 20.

22 Tate, *The Forlorn Demon,* 99–100.

23 Gilbert Chinard, "Literature and the Humanities," in Greene (ed.), *The Meaning of the Humanities,* 158.

24 J. Robert Oppenheimer, "The Open Mind," in *The Bulletin of the Atomic Scientists,* V, No. 1 (January, 1949), 5.

25 Kenneth Burke, *Permanence and Change* (New York: The New Republic, 1935), 71.

26 A. N. Whitehead, *The Aims of Education and Other Essays* (New York: The Macmillan Co., 1929), 19.

27 *Discours sur le Style,* trans. Lane Cooper, in *The Art of the Writer,* arr. and adapted by Lane Cooper (Ithaca, N.Y.: Cornell University Press, 1952), 153–54.

28 Cf. Marie Hochmuth, "The Criticism of Rhetoric," in *A History and Criticism of American Public Address,* ed. Marie K. Hochmuth (Vol. III; New York: Longmans, Green and Co., 1955), III, 21.

29 Donald Bryant, "Whither the Humanities?" *The Quarterly Journal of Speech,* XLII (December, 1956), 365.

30 John Ciardi, "Literature Undefended," *Saturday Review,* XLII (January 31, 1959), 22.

31 *Journals of Ralph Waldo Emerson,* eds. Edward Waldo Emerson and Waldo Emerson Forbes (10 vols.; Boston: Houghton Mifflin Co., 1912) VII, 503.

32 Cited in Robert D. Clark, "These Truths We Hold Self-Evident," *The Quarterly Journal of Speech,* XXXIV (December, 1948), 448.

33 Carl I. Hovland, Irving L. Janis, and Harold H. Kelley, *Communication and Persuasion* (New Haven: Yale University Press, 1953), Chs. 2, 3, 4. Cf. Paul Heinberg, "Scientific Research in Speech: Its Function and Frontiers," MS, State University of Iowa.

34   William Shakespeare, *Antony and Cleopatra,* Act V, Scene ii, line 95.
35   James Albert Winans, *Public Speaking* (Rev. ed.; N.Y.: The Century
     Co., 1915, 1917), 200.
36   John Livingston Lowes, "The Noblest Monument of English Prose," in
     Essays in Appreciation (Boston: Houghton Mifflin Co., 1936), 3–5.
37   Dwight MacDonald, "The Bible in Modern Undress," *The New Yorker*
     (November 14, 1953), 175.
38   Ralph Barton Perry, "A Definition of the Humanities," 22.
39   Kenneth Burke, *The Philosophy of Literary Form* (Baton Rouge, La.:
     Louisiana State University Press, 1941), 23.
40   Donald Bryant, "Whither the Humanities?" *loc. cit.,* 366.
41   Cited in Morris R. Cohen, *The Meaning of Human History* (La Salle,
     Ill.: Open Court Publishing Co., 1947), 224.

Chapter ii

1   Cited Chap. 1, n. 28.
2   *Selections from the Writings of Walter Savage Landor,* arr. and ed.,
     Sidney Colvin (London: Macmillan & Co., 1882), 276–77.
3   Helen F. North, "Rhetoric and Historiography," *The Quarterly Journal
     of Speech,* XLII (October, 1956), 234.
4   James T. Shotwell, *The History of History* (N.Y.: Columbia Univer-
     sity Press, 1939), I, 214–29; 256–69.
5   *Orator,* trans. H. M. Hubbell, xxxiv. 120.
6   *Brutus,* trans. J. S. Watson, xi. 42.
7   Shotwell, *The History of History,* 224.
8   Helen F. North, "Rhetoric and Historiography," *loc. cit.,* 237 ff.
9   R. C. Jebb, *The Attic Orators from Antiphon to Isacus* (2 vols., 1876;
     2d ed., 1893); cf. Shotwell, *The History of History,* 218.
10   Shotwell, *The History of History,* 219.
11   *Ibid.,* 219, 220.
12   *Ibid.,* 256; see, Cicero *De Oratore,* trans. J. S. Watson, II. xii–xv.
13   *De Oratore* II. xii.
14   *Ibid.,* II. xiii.
15   *Ibid.,* II. xv.
16   *The Institutio Oratoria of Quintilian,* trans. H. E. Butler (London:
     William Heinemann, 1936), XII. xi. 4.
17   Cited in Carl B. Cone, "Major Factors in the Rhetoric of Historians,"
     The Quarterly Journal of Speech, XXXIII (December, 1947), 442.
18   Josiah P. Quincy, "The Decline of Oratory," *Proceedings of the Massa-
     chusetts Historical Society,* Sec. Series, XV (1901–1902), 505.
19   Cited by Pieter Geyl, *Debates with Historians* (J. B. Wolters, Gro-
     ningen and Martinus Nijhoff: The Hague, Holland, 1955), 1.
20   Henry Morgenau, "The New View of Man in His Physical Environ-
     ment," *The Centennial Review of Arts & Science,* I (Winter, 1957),
     1–25.

21 Isaiah Berlin, *Historical Inevitability* (Auguste Compte Memorial Trust Lecture No. 1, delivered May 12, 1953 at London School of Economics and Political Science [London: Oxford University Press, 1954], 35.

22 James MacGregor Burns, *Roosevelt: The Lion and the Fox* (N.Y.: Harcourt, Brace and Co., 1956), 484.

23 Allan Nevins, "Is History Made by Heroes?" *Saturday Review,* XXXVIII (November 5, 1955), 44.

24 "The Autobiography," *The Writings of Benjamin Franklin* (N.Y.: MacMillan Co., 1905), I, 356–57.

25 Allan Nevins, *The Gateway to History* (Boston: D. C. Heath and Co., 1938), 225.

26 Hans Sperbner, "Fifty-Four Forty or Fight; Facts and Fictions," *American Speech,* XXXII (February, 1957), 5–11.

27 Carl Becker, "What is Historiography?" *The American Historical Review,* XLIV (October, 1938), 21.

28 Dixon Wecter, "History and How to Write It," *American Heritage,* VIII (August, 1957), 25.

29 Convention of Speech Association of the Eastern States, Sheraton-McAlpin Hotel, New York, April 13, 1957.

30 Robert J. Rayback.

31 Oscar Zeichner.

32 Robert J. Rayback, "What One Historian Expects from Rhetoricians," unpublished MS.

33 Charles Krey, "History and the Humanities," in *The Meaning of the Humanities,* ed. Theodore Meyer Green (Princeton, N.J.: Princeton University Press, 1938), 85.

34 Allan Nevins, "Is History Made by Heroes?" *loc. cit.,* 45.

35 O. Hobart Mowrer, "The Psychologist Looks at Language," *The American Psychologist,* IX (November, 1954), 660.

36 Burns, *Roosevelt: the Lion and the Fox.*

37 Richard Hofstadter, *The Age of Reform, from Bryan to F.D.R.* (N.Y.: Alfred A. Knopf, 1955), 6, 13, 23 ff.

38 Kenneth M. Stampp, *And the War Came* (Baton Rouge, La.: Louisiana State University Press, 1950), Ch. III.

39 Merle Curti, "The Great Mr. Locke: America's Philosopher, 1783–1861," *The Huntington Library Bulletin,* No. 11 (Cambridge, Mass.: Harvard University Press, April, 1937), 108, 109.

40 Herbert J. Muller, *The Uses of the Past* (N.Y.: Oxford University Press, 1953), 32, 33; see also, Carl L. Becker, "What Are Historical Facts?" *The Western Political Quarterly,* VIII, No. 3 (September, 1955), 327–40.

41 Ross Scanlan, "The Nazi Speakers' Complaints," *The Quarterly Journal of Speech,* XL (February, 1954), 1.

42 Adolph Hitler, *Mein Kampf,* trans. Ralph Manheim (Boston: Houghton Mifflin Co., 1943), 106–107.

43 Shotwell, *The History of History,* 259.

44 *Ibid.,* 214.
45 Zeichner, MS.
46 Shotwell, *The History of History,* 223.
47 Nevins, *The Gateway to History,* 28.
48 Dixon Wecter, "History and How to Write It," *loc. cit.,* 87.
49 Paul R. Beall, "Viper-Crusher Turns Dragon-Slayer," *The Quarterly Journal of Speech,* XXXVIII (February, 1952), 52.
50 Shotwell, *The History of History,* 9.
51 Cited by Muller, *The Uses of the Past,* 31.
52 *Ibid.,* 31.
53 Charles A. Beard, "Written History as an Act of Faith," *The American Historical Review,* XXXIX, No. 2 (January, 1934), 219–29.
54 Muller, *The Uses of the Past,* 31.
55 Charles Krey, "History and the Humanities," 87.
56 Learned Hand, "Mr. Justice Brandeis," in Irving Dilliard, ed., *The Spirit of Liberty: Papers and Addresses of Learned Hand* (N.Y.: Alfred A. Knopf, Inc., 1959), 128, 129.
57 Muller, *The Uses of the Past,* 29.
58 Cited in Donald L. Clark, "The Place of Rhetoric in a Liberal Education," *The Quarterly Journal of Speech,* XXXVI (October, 1950), 294.
59 Robert D. Clark, "The Influence of the Frontier on American Political Oratory," *The Quarterly Journal of Speech,* XXVIII (October, 1942), 282–89.
60 Edward Everett Dale, "The Speech of the Frontier," *The Quarterly Journal of Speech,* XXVII (October, 1941), 353–63.
61 Irving Dilliard, *The Spirit of Liberty,* vi.
62 *The Institutio Oratoria of Quintilian* XII. xi. 4.

Chapter III

1 Robert Morell Schmitz, *Hugh Blair* (New York: King's Crown Press, 1948), 49.
2 Cicero *Brutus,* trans. J. S. Watson, XII.
3 *Ibid.,* XII.
4 Claude M. Fuess, "Ghosts in the White House," *American Heritage,* X (December, 1958), 46.
5 Louis A. Mallory, "Patrick Henry," in *A History and Criticism of American Public Address,* ed. William Norwood Brigance (2 vols.; N.Y.: McGraw-Hill, 1943), II, 590; see also, William Wirt, *Sketches of the Life and Character of Patrick Henry* (Philadelphia: Thomas, Cowperthwait & Co., 1839), 138–42.
6 Fuess, "Ghosts in the White House," *loc. cit.,* 46.
7 *Ibid.,* 46.
8 Homer Carey Hockett, *The Critical Method in Historical Research and Writing* (A Rewritten and expanded ed. of *Introduction to Research in American History* [N.Y.: The Macmillan Co., 1955], 25.

9   *Ibid.,* p. 25, n. 13.

10 Cited in Fuess, "Ghosts in the White House," *loc. cit.,* 97.

11 *Ibid.,* 47.

12 Quoted in Russel Windes, Jr., and James A. Robinson, "Public Address in the Career of Adlai E. Stevenson," *The Quarterly Journal of Speech,* XLII (October, 1956), 229.

13 Laura Crowell, "The Building of the 'Four Freedoms' Speech," *Speech Monographs,* XXII, No. 5 (November, 1955), 266–83; see also, Robert E. Sherwood, *Roosevelt and Hopkins* (N.Y.: Harper & Brothers, 1948), 212–19; also, Earnest Brandenburg and Waldo W. Braden, "Franklin Delano Roosevelt," *A History and Criticism of American Public Address,* ed. Marie Kathryn Hochmuth (Vol. III, N.Y.: Longmans, Greene and Co., 1955), III, 464–82.

14 Quoted in *The New Yorker,* February 23, 1952, p. 23.

15 *Ibid.*

16 *Ibid.*

17 *Newsweek,* XXXIX (January-March, 1952), 71. (February 4, issue).

18 *Ibid.*

19 Charles Michelson, *The Ghost Talks* (N.Y.: G. P. Putnam's Sons, 1944), 218.

20 *Ibid.,* 193.

21 Cited in Lloyd I. Watkins, "Lord Brougham's Authorship of Rhetorical Articles in the *Edinburgh Review," The Quarterly Journal of Speech,* XLII (February, 1956), 55.

22 Hockett, *The Critical Method . . .,* 24.

23 *Ibid.,* p. 24, n. 12.

24 Robert T. Oliver, "Arthur H. Vandenberg," *The Quarterly Journal of Speech,* XXXIV (October, 1948), 320.

25 Douglass Cater, "Government by Publicity," *The Reporter,* XX (March 19, 1959), 15, 16.

26 Earnest R. May, "Whodunit?" *The New Republic,* CXXXVI (April 22, 1957), 13, 14.

27 Hockett, *The Critical Method . . .,* 63.

28 *Ibid.,* 63.

29 "The Intellectual Gigolo Strikes Back," *The Articulates,* ed. John M. Henry, with introduction by Virgil M. Hancher, President of State University of Iowa (Indianapolis, N.Y.: The Bobbs-Merrill Company, Inc., 1957), 43–48.

30 "The Intellectual Gigolo Strikes Back," Henry (ed.), *The Articulates, passim,* 43–48.

31 Orville Hitchcock, review of *The Articulates,* in *The Quarterly Journal of Speech,* XLV (April, 1959), 218, 219.

32 *A Discourse in Commemoration of the Lives and Services of John Adams & Thomas Jefferson, Delivered in Faneuil Hall, Boston, August 2, 1826* (Boston: Cummings, Hilliard & Co., 1826), 34.

33 Schmitz, *Hugh Blair,* 49.

34 Cited in Fuess, "Ghosts in the White House," *loc. cit.,* 99.
35 "The Intellectual Gigolo Strikes Back," Henry (ed.), *The Articulates,* 47.
36 Cited in Fuess, "Ghosts in the White House," *loc. cit.,* 99.

Chapter IV

1 Chauncey A. Goodrich, *Select British Eloquence* (N.Y.: Harper & Brothers, 1872), Preface, iii.
2 *The Life and Works of Lord Macaulay* (Edinburgh ed.; N.Y.: Longmans, Greene, and Co., 1897), VII, 378.
3 *American Orations: Studies in American Political History,* edited with an introduction by Alexander Johnston; re-edited with historical and textual notes by James Albert Woodburn (4 vols.; N.Y. and London: G. P. Putnam's Sons, The Knickerbocker Press, 1896).
4 *The World's Orators,* ed. Guy Carlton Lee (10 vols.; Daniel Webster ed.; N.Y. and London: G. P. Putnam's Sons, Co., 1899, 1903).
5 *The World's Best Orations, from the Earliest Period to the Present Time,* ed. David Brewer (11 vols.; St. Louis and Chicago: Ferd. P. Kaiser, 1899).
6 *Modern Eloquence,* ed. Thomas B. Reed (15 vols.; Philadelphia: John D. Morris & Co., 1900).
7 *Masterpieces of American Eloquence,* Christian Herald selection with Introduction by Julia Ward Howe (N.Y.: The Christian Herald, 1900).
8 *The Library of Oratory,* ed. Chauncey M. Depew (New York and Chicago: E. R. DuMont, 1902).
9 Johnston and Woodburn, (eds.), *American Orations,* I, "Introductory," xiv.
10 *Ibid.,* Preface to the revised edition, vii.
11 *Ibid.,* x.
12 *Ibid.,* x.
13 Lee (ed.), *The World's Orators,* I, vii.
14 *Ibid.,* I, vii.
15 *Ibid.,* I, vii.
16 *Ibid.,* VIII, 3.
17 *Ibid.,* VIII, 2.
18 *Ibid.,* VIII, 2.
19 *Ibid.,* VIII, 3.
20 *Ibid.,* VIII, 21.
21 *Ibid.,* VIII, 29.
22 *Ibid.,* VIII, 113, 114.
23 *Ibid.,* VIII, 159.
24 *Ibid.,* VIII, 237.
25 Brewer (ed.), *The World's Best Orations,* Flysheet, unnumbered.
26 *Ibid.,* I, ix.

27   *Ibid.,* I, ix.
28   *Ibid.,* I, ix.
29   *Ibid.,* I, x.
30   *Ibid.,* I, xi.
31   *Ibid.,* I, xi.
32   *Ibid.,* I, x, xi.
33   *Ibid.,* I, xi.
34   Reed (ed.), *Modern Eloquence,* I, xiii.
35   *Ibid.,* I, v.
36   *Ibid.,* I, v.
37   *Ibid.,* I, xi.
38   *Ibid.,* I, xiii.
39   *Ibid.,* I, xiii.
40   *Ibid.,* I, v.
41   *Ibid.,* I, xiv.
42   *Ibid.,* I, iv.
43   Christian Herald Selection, *Masterpieces of American Eloquence,* 2.
44   *Ibid.,* 4.
45   *Ibid.,* 1.
46   *Ibid.,* 3.
47   *Ibid.,* 3.
48   *Ibid.,* 1.
49   *Ibid.,* 24.
50   *Ibid.,* 24.
51   Depew (ed.), *Library of Oratory,* I, iv.
52   *Ibid.,* I, iv.
53   *Ibid.,* I, iv.
54   *Ibid.,* I, i.
55   *Ibid.,* I, iii, iv.
56   Joseph Moore McConnell, *Southern Orators: Speeches and Orations* (N.Y.: The Macmillan Company, 1910), vii, viii.
57   Joseph Villiers Denney, *American Public Addresses* (Chicago: Scott, Foresman and Co., 1910), Preface, iii.
58   *Ibid.,* iii, iv.
59   *Ibid.,* viii–32.
60   *Classified Models of Speech Composition,* comp. by James Milton O'Neill (N.Y.: The Century Co., 1922), Preface, ix.
61   *Ibid.,* ix.
62   Warren Choate Shaw, *History of American Oratory* (Indianapolis: The Bobbs-Merrill Co., 1928), iii.
63   *Ibid.,* iii.
64   *Ibid.,* iii, iv.
65   *Ibid.,* iv.
66   *Ibid.,* iii.
67   William Norwood Brigance, *Classified Speech Models of Eighteen Forms of Public Address* (N.Y.: F. S. Grofts & Co., 1930), vii.

68 *Ibid.,* vii, viii.

69 *Ibid.,* viii.

70 *Ibid.,* vii.

71 Herbert A. Wichelns, "The Literary Criticism of Oratory," *Studies in Rhetoric and Public Speaking in Honor of James Albert Winans* (New York: The Century Co., 1925), 209.

72 *A History and Criticism of American Public Address,* ed., William Norwood Brigance (2 vols.; N.Y.: McGraw-Hill Book Co., 1943), I, vii.

73 *Ibid.,* I, vii.

74 *Ibid.,* I, viii.

75 Donald C. Bryant, "Some Problems of Scope and Method in Rhetorical Scholarship," *The Quarterly Journal of Speech,* XXIII (April, 1937), 182, 183.

76 *Ibid.,* 187, 188.

77 S. Judson Grandell, "Social Control Techniques in the Speeches of the Women's Christian Temperance Union" (unpublished Ph.D. Dissertation, Northwestern University, 1946).

78 Leland M. Griffin, "The Antimasonic Persuasion: A Study of Public Address in the American Antimasonic Movement, 1826–1838" (unpublished Ph.D. Dissertation, Cornell University, 1950).

79 Ernest Wrage, "Public Address: A Study in Social and Intellectual History," *The Quarterly Journal of Speech,* XXXIII (December, 1947), 456.

80 *Ibid.,* 451.

81 *Ibid.,* 454.

82 Merle Curti, "The Great Mr. Locke: America's Philosopher, 1783–1861," *The Huntington Library Bulletin,* No. 11 (April, 1937), 109.

83 Max Lerner, *Ideas are Weapons* (N.Y.: The Viking Press, 1939), 6.

84 A. Craig Baird, *American Public Addresses, 1740–1952* (N.Y.: McGraw-Hill, 1956).

85 Alexander M. Drummond and Everett Lee Hunt, *Persistent Questions In Public Discussion* (New York and London: The Century Company, 1924).

86 Harold F. Harding, *The Age of Danger* (N.Y.: Random House, 1952), Preface, v, vi.

87 Wayland Maxfield Parrish and Marie Hochmuth, *American Speeches* (New York: Longmans, Greene and Co., 1954).

88 John T. Flanagan, "Three Allied Arts," *The Quarterly Journal of Speech,* XXXIV (February, 1948), 35.

Chapter v

1   $\mathbb{A}$ristophanes, *The Frogs,* trans. J. Hookham Frere, lines 1381–85.
2   William K. Wimsatt, Jr., and Cleanth Brooks, *Literary Criticism: A Short History* (N.Y.: Alfred A. Knopf, 1957), 4.
3   Cicero *Brutus,* trans. by J. S. Watson, XVII.
4   Barnet Baskerville, "Some American Critics of Public Address, 1850–1900," *Speech Monographs,* XVII (March, 1950), 1–23.
5   Herbert A. Wichelns, "The Literary Criticism of Oratory," in *Studies in Rhetoric and Public Speaking in Honor of James Albert Winans* (N.Y.: The Century Co., 1925), 181–216.
6   Lester Thonssen and A. Craig Baird, *Speech Criticism* (N.Y.: The Ronald Press, 1948).
7   Ed. William Norwood Brigance (2 vols; N.Y.: McGraw-Hill, 1943); ed. by Marie Hochmuth (Vol. III; N.Y.: Longmans, Greene & Co., 1955).
8   "Demosthenes," in *Plutarch's Lives,* trans. called Dryden's; rev. by A. H. Clough (5 vols.; N.Y.: Bigelow, Brown & Co., 1911), V, 3.
9   Allen Tate, "Is Literary Criticism Possible?" in *The Forlorn Demon: Didactic and Critical Essays* (Chicago: Regnery, 1953), 96–111.
10 Loren D. Reid, "The Perils of Rhetorical Criticism," *The Quarterly Journal of Speech,* XXX (December, 1944), 416–22.
11 Frederick W. Haberman, "General MacArthur's Speech: A Symposium of Critical Comment," *The Quarterly Journal of Speech,* XXXVI (October, 1951), 321–31.
12 Karl Wallace, "On the Criticism of the MacArthur Speech," *The Quarterly Journal of Speech,* XXXIX (February, 1953), 69–74.
13 Paul R. Beall, "Viper-Crusher Turns Dragon-Slayer," *The Quarterly Journal of Speech,* XXXVIII (February, 1952), 51–56.
14 Oscar Zeichner, Paper presented at the Convention of the Speech Association of the Eastern States, Sheraton-McAlpin Hotel, New York, April 13, 1957, MS.
15 Vernon Louis Parrington, *The Romantic Revolution in America* in *Main Currents in American Thought* (3 vols.; N.Y.: Harcourt, Brace & Co., 1927–30), II, 158.
16 *Abraham Lincoln: His Speeches and Writings,* ed. Roy P. Basler (Cleveland: The World Publishing Co., 1946), 28.
17 I. A. Richards, *The Philosophy of Rhetoric* (N.Y.: Oxford University Press, 1936), 3.
18 Charles Sears Baldwin, *Ancient Rhetoric and Poetic* (N.Y.: The MacMillan Co., 1924), 247.
19 Richard Weaver, *The Ethics of Rhetoric* (Chicago: Henry Regnery Co., 1953), 25.
20 Barnet Baskerville, "Emerson as a Critic of Oratory," *The Southern Speech Journal,* XVIII (March, 1953), 161.

21 A. Craig Baird, *American Public Addresses, 1740–1952*, (N.Y.: McGraw-Hill Book Co., 1956), 14.

22 Kenneth Burke, "The Rhetoric of Hitler's Battle," in his *The Philosophy of Literary Form*, 191.

23 Paul Franklin Baum, *The Other Harmony of Prose* (North Carolina: Duke University Press, 1952), 3.

24 Ralph Waldo Emerson, "Art," *Essays: First and Second Series* (Havard ed.; Boston: Houghton Mifflin Co., 1929), First Series, 355.

25 Alfred North Whitehead, *The Aims of Education and Other Essays* (N.Y.: The Macmillan Co., 1929), 19.

26 London *Observer*, October 31, 1952.

27 Woodrow Wilson, *An Old Master and Other Political Essays* (N.Y.: Charles Scribner's Sons, 1893), 21.

28 *Ibid.*, 22.

29 Robert A. Hall, Jr., *Leave Your Language Alone* (Ithaca, N.Y.: Linguistica, 1950).

30 *Ibid.*, 236.

31 Edward J. Hegarty, *How to Write A Speech* (N.Y.: McGraw-Hill Book Co., 1951), 55, 56.

32 *Ibid.*, 64.

33 E. Jordan, *Essays in Criticism* (Chicago: University of Chicago Press, 1952), 193.

34 Helen Wheatley Schrader, "A Linguistic Approach to the Study of Rhetorical Style" (unpublished Ph.D. dissertation, Northwestern University, 1949), 17.

35 *Ibid.*, 15.

36 Harold D. Lasswell, Nathan Leites, and Associates, *Language of Politics* (N.Y.: George W. Stewart, Publisher, Inc., 1949), 38.

37 George A. Miller, *Language and Communication* (N.Y.: McGraw-Hill Book Co., 1951), xi.

38 Donald C. Bryant, "On Style," *Western Speech*, XXI (Spring, 1957), 110.

39 John Ciardi, "Literature Undefended," *Saturday Review*, XLII (January 31, 1959), 22.

40 Ross Scanlan, "The Nazi Rhetorician," *The Quarterly Journal of Speech*, XXXVII (December, 1951), 430–40; see also, "The Nazi Speakers' Complaints," XL (February, 1954), 1–14.

41 Cicero *De Oratore*, trans. by J. S. Watson, II. xx.

42 Ralph Waldo Emerson, "Nominalist and Realist," *Essays*, Second Series, 230, 231.

Chapter vi

1   $\mathbf{M}$arie Hochmuth, "Kenneth Burke and the 'New Rhetoric,'"
    The Quarterly Journal of Speech, XXXVIII (April, 1952), 133–44.
2   Marie Hochmuth, "I. A. Richards and the 'New Rhetoric,'" *The Quar-
    terly Journal of Speech,* XLIV (February, 1958), 1–16.
3   Saul Bellow, "Deep Readers of the World, Beware," *The New York
    Times Book Review,* Sec. 7 (February 15, 1959), 1 ff.
4   Kenneth Burke, *Linguistic Approach to Problems of Education,* Off-
    print from the Fifty-fourth Yearbook of the National Society for the
    Study of Education, Part I, *Modern Philosophies and Education,* 1955
    (Chicago, Ill.: National Society for the Study of Education, 1955).
5   W. H. Auden, "A Grammar of Assent," *The New Republic,* CV (July
    14, 1941), 59; see also, Malcolm Cowley, "Prolegomena to Kenneth
    Burke," *The New Republic,* CXXII (July 5, 1950), 18, 19.
6   Charles Morris, "The Strategy of Kenneth Burke," *The Nation,* CLXIII
    (July 27, 1946); see also, *Signs, Language and Behavior* (N.Y.: Pren-
    tice-Hall, Inc., 1946), vii, 265.
7   Burke has recently published a volume entitled *The Rhetoric of Reli-
    gion* (Boston: Beacon Press, 1961).
8   Professor Waldo Braden, Department of Speech, Louisiana State Uni-
    versity.
9   Professor-emeritus Claude Wise, Department of Speech, Louisiana State
    University.
10 Kenneth Burke, *A Rhetoric of Motives* (N.Y.: Prentice-Hall, Inc.,
    1950), 146.
11 *Ibid.,* 271.
12 *Ibid.,* 43.
13 *Ibid.,* 172.
14 Bronislaw Malinowski, "The Problem of Meaning in Primitive Lan-
    guages," Supplement I, in C. K. Ogden and I. A. Richards, *The Mean-
    ing of Meaning* (N.Y.: Harcourt, Brace and Co., Inc., 1953), 296–336.
15 *Ibid.,* 48 ff.
16 Burke, *A Rhetoric of Motives,* 42.
17 Professor-emeritus Giles Gray, Department of Speech, Louisiana State
    University.
18 Burke, *A Rhetoric of Motives,* 43–44.
19 Kenneth Burke, "Rhetoric—Old and New," *The Journal of General
    Education,* V (April, 1951), 203.
20 Burke, *A Rhetoric of Motives,* 21.
21 Kenneth Burke, *A Grammar of Motives* (N.Y.: Prentice-Hall, Inc.,
    1945), 21–58.
22 Cf. Aristotle *Rhetorica,* trans. by W. Rhys Roberts, 1415b. 28.
23 Kenneth Burke, *Permanence and Change* (rev. ed.: Los Altos, Calif.:
    Hermes Publications, 1954), 50.

24 Kenneth Burke, *Linguistic Approach to the Problems of Education*, 259.
25 Kenneth Burke, *The Philosophy of Literary Form*, 20 ff.
26 Ogden and Richards, *The Meaning of Meaning*, 55.

Chapter VII

1   Cf. Marie Hochmuth, "I. A. Richards and the 'New Rhetoric,' " *The Quarterly Journal of Speech*, XLIV (February, 1958), 1–16.
2   I. A. Richards, *The Philosophy of Rhetoric* (N.Y.: Oxford University Press, 1936), 3.
3   Learned Hand, "The Preservation of Personality," An Address delivered at Commencement Ceremonies at Bryn Mawr College, Bryn Mawr, Pennsylvania, June 2, 1927, in *The Spirit of Liberty*, ed., Irving Dilliard (N.Y.: Alfred A. Knopf, Inc., 1959), 24.
4   D. W. Harding, "I. A. Richards," *Scrutiny*, I (March, 1933), 336.
5   Charles Morris, *Signs, Language and Behavior* (N.Y.: Prentice-Hall, Inc., 1946), vii, 265.
6   Ogden and Richards, *The Meaning of Meaning*, 11.
7   Richards, *The Philosophy of Rhetoric*, 24.
8   I. A. Richards, *Interpretation in Teaching* (N.Y.: Harcourt Brace and Co., 1938), 11.
9   Aristotle *Rhetorica*, trans. W. Rhys Roberts, I.2.1355b.
10 Richard Whately, *Elements of Rhetoric* (Reprinted from the 7th ed.; London: Longmans, Greene, Reader, and Dyer, 1866), 113.
11 I. A. Richards, *Speculative Instruments* (Chicago: The University of Chicago Press, 1955), 159.
12 Richards, *The Philosophy of Rhetoric*, 24.
13 Richards, *Speculative Instruments*, 166.
14 *Ibid.*, 131.
15 *Ibid.*, 52.
16 Richards, *The Philosophy of Rhetoric*, 39.
17 Richard Murphy, "The Ethics of Debating Both Sides," *The Speech Teacher*, VI (January, 1957), 1–9.
18 Whately, *Elements of Rhetoric*, 3.
19 Richards, *The Philosophy of Rhetoric*, 5, 7, 8, 9.
20 Arthur Bestor, *Educational Wastelands* (Urbana, Ill.: The University of Illinois Press, 1953), 62, 63.
21 H. M. McLuhan, "Poetic vs. Rhetorical Exegesis," *Sewanee Review*, LII (Winter, 1944), 266–76.
22 Walter J. Ong, S.J., *Ramus: Method, and the Decay of Dialogue* (Cambridge, Mass.: Harvard University Press, 1958).
23 George Campbell, *The Philosophy of Rhetoric* (7th ed.; London: Printed for William Baynes and Son, 1823), 7.
24 Richards, *Interpretation in Teaching*, 12.

25 Campbell, *The Philosophy of Rhetoric,* Bk. I, Ch. 1, p. 13.
26 Richards, *Interpretation in Teaching,* 12, 13.
27 Richards, *The Philosophy of Rhetoric,* 3.
28 Richards, *Interpretation in Teaching,* 14, 15.
29 Richards, *The Philosophy of Rhetoric,* 7.
30 Cf. Donald Lee Torrence, "A Philosophy for Rhetoric Constructed from the Writings of Bertrand Russell" (unpublished Ph.D. dissertation, University of Illinois, 1957).
31 I. A. Richards, *Science and Poetry* (N.Y.: W. W. Norton & Co., Inc., 1926), 67, 70, 71.
32 I. A. Richards, *Practical Criticism* (N.Y.: Harcourt, Brace and Co., 1954), 5, 6, 8.
33 B. F. Skinner, *Verbal Behavior* (N.Y.: Appleton-Century-Crofts, Inc., 1957), 4, 5.
34 Morris, *Signs, Language and Behavior,* 69 ff.
35 Donald Lemen Clark, "The Place of Rhetoric in a Liberal Education," *The Quarterly Journal of Speech,* XXXVI (October, 1950), 291–95, *passim.*
36 Richards, *The Philosophy of Rhetoric,* 9, 10.
37 Richards, *Practical Criticism,* 180, 181, 182, 183, 207.
38 *Ibid.,* 11.
39 Richards, *Speculative Instruments,* 122.
40 I. A. Richards, *Principles of Literary Criticism* (N.Y.: Harcourt, Brace and Co., 1952), 255.
41 *Speech Monographs,* XXV (June, 1958), 114.
42 *Speech Monographs,* XXIV (June, 1957), 114.

Chapter VIII

1   **B**ernard Mandeville, *The Fable of the Bees,* Part II [1729], ed. F. B. Kaye (Oxford: The Clarendon Press, 1924), II, 342.
2   *The Quarterly Journal of Speech,* XXXV (December, 1949), 510.
3   Bernard Shaw, *Sixteen Self Sketches* (N.Y.: Dodd, Mead & Co., 1949), 193.
4   New York *Times,* October 12, 1931, p. 30, col. 2; cf. *Bernard Shaw: Platform and Pulpit,* ed. Dan H. Laurence (N.Y.: Hill and Wang, 1961), 226–34.
5   *Public Opinion,* April 3, 1875, cited in Archibald Henderson, *Man of the Century* (N.Y.: Appleton-Century-Crofts, Inc., 1956), 47, 48.
6   Henderson, *Man of the Century,* 135-39.
7   George Bernard Shaw, *Immaturity* (Standard Edition: London: Constable and Co., 1931), Preface, xl.
8   Henderson, *Man of the Century,* 215–17; cf. Bernard Shaw, *Sixteen Self Sketches,* 96.

9   Edward R. Pease, *The History of the Fabian Society* (New and rev. ed.: N.Y.: International Publishers, 1926), 37.
10 *Immaturity,* Preface, p. xxvii; cf. Henderson, *Man of the Century,* 132–60.
11 Pease, *History of the Fabian Society,* 77.
12 George Bernard Shaw, "The Fabian Society" in *Essays in Fabian Socialism* (Standard ed.; London: Constable and Co., 1932), 146.
13 Archibald Henderson, *Bernard Shaw: Playboy and Prophet* (N.Y.: D. Appleton and Co., 1932), 124.
14 S. Winsten, *Days with Bernard Shaw* (London: Hutchinson and Co., 1948), 20.
15 Beatrice Webb, *Our Partnership,* eds. Barbara Drake and Margaret I. Cole (N.Y.: Longmans, Greene and Co., 1948), 447.
16 George Bernard Shaw, *Our Theatres in the Nineties* (3 vols.; Standard ed.: London: Constable and Co., 1932), III, 385.
17 Shaw, *Sixteen Self Sketches,* 159.
18 G. K. Chesterton, *George Bernard Shaw* (New York: Hill and Wang, 1958), 57.
19 *Bernard Shaw and Mrs. Patrick Campbell: Their Correspondence,* ed. Alan Dent (London: Victor Gollancz, Ltd., 1952), 58.
20 *Three Plays for Puritans* (London: Constable and Co., 1931), Preface, xxi; see also, Hesketh Pearson, *G.B.S.: A Full Length Portrait* (Reprint ed.; N.Y.: Garden City Publishing Co., Inc., 1946), 52.
21 Shaw, *Sixteen Self Sketches,* 130.
22 *Ibid.,* 95, 96.
23 *Industrial Remuneration Conference: The Report of the Proceedings and Papers Read in Prince's Hall, Piccadilly* (London: Cassell & Co., Ltd., 1885), 400. Cf. Hesketh Pearson, *G.B.S.: A Full Length Portrait,* 62.
24 *Ibid.;* cf. Pearson, *G.B.S.,* 62.
25 George Bernard Shaw, "The Fabian Society," 144.
26 Pease, *History of the Fabian Society,* 94, 95.
27 *Ibid.,* 282.
28 Eric Bentley, *Bernard Shaw* ("The Makers of Modern Literature," Amended ed. [Norfolk, Conn.: New Directions Books, 1957]), 24.
29 Cf. Maurice Colbourne, *The Real Bernard Shaw* (N.Y.: Dodd, Mead and Co., 1940), 132–49.
30 Holbrook Jackson, *Bernard Shaw* (2nd ed.; London: Grant Richards, 1909), 66, 67.
31 Shaw, *Our Theatres in the Nineties,* II, 195.
32 Henderson, *Man of the Century,* 298.
33 *Ibid.,* 386.
34 G. Bernard Shaw, "The Ideal of Citizenship," delivered at meeting of The Progressive League, City Temple, October 11, 1909, in R. J. Campbell, *The New Theology,* (Popular ed.; London: Mills and Boon, n.d. [January, 1910]), 257–68.

35 Chesterton, *George Bernard Shaw,* 50.
36 *Ibid.,* 47.
37 J. S. Collis, *Shaw* (London: Jonathan Cape, Ltd., 1925), 94, 95.
38 Webb, *Our Partnership,* 284.
39 *Times* (London), March 8, 1906, p. 10, col. f.
40 G. Bernard Shaw, "The Ideal of Citizenship," 266.
41 *Ibid.*
42 Clarence Rook, "George Bernard Shaw," *The Chap-Book,* November 1, 1896, p. 539; see also, Henderson, *Man of the Century,* 196.
43 S. Winsten, *Days With Bernard Shaw,* 196.
44 Henderson, *Playboy and Prophet,* 341.
45 George Bernard Shaw, "A Little Talk on America," Address delivered October 11, 1931 from Savoy Hill, broadcast to America (London: Published by Friends of the Soviet Union, 1931).
46 Bernard Shaw, "Are We Heading for War?" Speech delivered by Mr. Bernard Shaw in the B.B.C.'s "Whither Britain" series (London: Victoria House Printing Co., Ltd.; Published by the Labour Party, n.d.).
47 Henderson, *Playboy and Prophet,* 269; also, Henderson, *Man of the Century,* 173.
48 Cf. his "The Fabian Society," 144, 145.
49 Collis, *Shaw,* 148.
50 *Immaturity,* Preface, xxxix.
51 "Epistle Dedicatory to Arthur Bingham Walkley," *Man and Superman* (Standard ed.; Constable & Co., 1931), xxxiv–xxxv.
52 *Back to Methuselah* (Standard ed.; London: Constable & Co., Ltd., 1931), Preface, xxv.
53 *Sixteen Self Sketches,* 37.
54 Chicago *Sunday Tribune,* September 25, 1949, p. 20.
55 Chesterton, *George Bernard Shaw,* 67, 68.
56 *Sixteen Self Sketches,* 196.
57 Blanche Patch, *Thirty Years with G.B.S.* (London: Victor Gollancz, Ltd., 1951), 29 ff.
58 *Pygmalion,* Act I.
59 *Sixteen Self Sketches,* 104.
60 Archibald Henderson, *George Bernard Shaw: His Life and Works* (Cincinnati: Stewart & Kidd, 1911), 500.
61 Laurence Housman, "G.B.S. and the Victorians," in *G.B.S. 90,* ed. S. Winsten (N.Y.: Dodd, Mead and Co., 1946), 55.
62 *Back to Methuselah,* Preface, xlii.
63 C. E. M. Joad, *Shaw* (London: Gollancz, 1949), 29, 70, 71.
64 George Bernard Shaw, "Foundation Oration," delivered in the Botanical Theatre, University College, London, March 18, 1920 (London: University College Union Society, University of London, 1920).
65 See Edmund Wilson, "Bernard Shaw at Eighty," in *George Bernard Shaw: A Critical Survey,* ed. by Louis Kronenberger (Cleveland: The World Publishing Co., 1953), 126–52.
66 Chesterton, *George Bernard Shaw,* 21.

Index